Teaching the Common Core Math Standards with Hands-On Activities, Grades 3–5

Judith A. Muschla

Gary Robert Muschla

Erin Muschla-Berry

JB JOSSEY-BASS™

A Wiley Brand

Cover design by Wiley
Cover art by Thinkstock
Cover image by © iStockphoto.com/jenifoto

Published by Jossey-Bass
A Wiley Brand
One Montgomery Street, Suite 1000, San Francisco, CA 94101-4594 www.josseybass.com

Jossey-Bass books and products are available through most bookstores. To contact Jossey-Bass directly call our Customer Care Department within the U.S. at 800-956-7739, outside the U.S. at 317-572-3986, or fax 317-572-4002.

Wiley publishes in a variety of print and electronic formats and by print-on-demand. Some material included with standard print versions of this book may not be included in e-books or in print-on-demand. If this book refers to media such as a CD or DVD that is not included in the version you purchased, you may download this material at http://booksupport.wiley.com. For more information about Wiley products, visit www.wiley.com.

Library of Congress Cataloging-in-Publication Data
Library of Congress Cataloging-in-Publication Data has been applied for and is on file with the Library of Congress.
ISBN 978-1-118-71033-3 (pbk); ISBN 978-1-118-83552-4 (ebk); ISBN 978-1-118-71044-9 (ebk)

Printed in the United States of America
FIRST EDITION

PB Printing   10 9 8 7 6 5 4 3 2

JOSSEY-BASS TEACHER

Jossey-Bass Teacher provides educators with practical knowledge and tools to create a positive and lifelong impact on student learning. We offer classroom-tested and research-based teaching resources for a variety of grade levels and subject areas. Whether you are an aspiring, new, or veteran teacher, we want to help you make every teaching day your best.

From ready-to-use classroom activities to the latest teaching framework, our value-packed books provide insightful, practical, and comprehensive materials on the topics that matter most to K–12 teachers. We hope to become your trusted source for the best ideas from the most experienced and respected experts in the field.

Other Math Books by the Muschlas

- *Geometry Teacher's Activities Kit: Ready-to-Use Lessons and Worksheets for Grades 6–12*

- *Math Smart!: Over 220 Ready-to-Use Activities to Motivate and Challenge Students, Grades 6–12*

- *Algebra Teacher's Activities Kit: 150 Ready-to-Use Activities with Real-World Applications*

- *Math Games: 180 Reproducible Activities to Motivate, Excite, and Challenge Students, Grades 6–12*

- *The Math Teacher's Book of Lists, 2nd Edition*

- *The Math Teacher's Problem-a-Day, Grades 4–8: Over 180 Reproducible Pages of Quick Skill Builders*

- *Hands-On Math Projects with Real-Life Applications, Grades 3–5*

- *Hands-On Math Projects with Real-Life Applications: Grades 6–12, 2nd Edition*

- *Math Teacher's Survival Guide: Practical Strategies, Management Techniques, and Reproducibles for New and Experienced Teachers, Grades 5–12*

- *The Algebra Teacher's Guide to Reteaching Essential Concepts and Skills: 150 Mini-Lessons for Correcting Common Mistakes*

- *Teaching the Common Core Math Standards with Hands-On Activities, Grades 6–8*

- *Math Starters: 5- to 10-Minute Activities Aligned with the Common Core Math Standards, Grades 6–12, 2nd Edition*

ABOUT THIS BOOK

The Common Core State Standards Initiative for Mathematics identifies the concepts, skills, and practices that students should understand and apply at their grade level. Mastery of these Standards at the elementary level will enable students to successfully move on to middle school mathematics.

Teaching the Common Core Math Standards with Hands-On Activities, Grades 3–5 offers a variety of activities that support instruction of the Standards. The Table of Contents provides a list of the Standards and supporting activities, enabling you to easily find material for developing your lessons. The book is divided into three sections:

- Section 1: Standards and Activities for Grade 3

- Section 2: Standards and Activities for Grade 4

- Section 3: Standards and Activities for Grade 5

The book is designed for easy implementation. The activities build on concepts and skills that you have already taught and expand the scope of your instruction through reinforcement and enrichment. Each activity is preceded by the Domain, which is a group of related Standards, followed by the specific Standard that the activity addresses. For example, "Operations and Algebraic Thinking: 4.OA.3" refers to the Domain, which is Operations and Algebraic Thinking, Grade 4, and Standard 3. Next, you will find background information on the topic, the title and a brief summary of the activity, special materials needed for the activity, and any special preparation that is necessary. Where applicable, the activities are identified with icons that indicate a major component of the activity will be cooperative learning 🤝, technology 💻, or real-world focus 🌐. All of the activities include specific steps for implementation, and many include reproducibles.

Each standard for grades 3–5 is supported by at least one activity. The typical activity can be completed in a single class period and focuses on application of concepts or skills, demonstration of understanding, or communication about math. Students may be required to solve problems; create mathematical models, charts, and graphs; conduct investigations with both physical and virtual manipulatives; play mathematical games; and write problems and explanations. Many of the activities are open-ended; however, an answer key is provided for those problems requiring specific answers.

Because many activities offer multiple avenues for development and learning, we encourage you to modify them in ways that best meet the needs of your students. For example, in some activities where we suggest that students work in pairs or groups of three, you may feel that your students will gain the most from the activity by working individually. Conversely, for some activities, rather than having students work individually, you may find it more practical to have them work with a partner. For activities that require the use of computers and the Internet, instead of having students work at a Web site on their own, you may prefer to use a computer and digital projector to lead your students through the Web site in a whole-class activity. You should present each activity in a manner that satisfies your objectives and is appropriate for the capabilities of your students.

To enhance your instruction of the activities, consider the following:

- Use a variety of instructional tools, such as traditional boards, whiteboards, overhead projectors, computers, scanners, digital projectors, and document cameras to present material in an effective and interesting manner.

- Preview every Web site and work through any exercises so that you are better able to offer guidance during the activity.

- Demonstrate the use of Web sites to your students before they begin working at the site.

- Paste the URLs of Web sites in your browser to make the Web site easy to access.

- For activities that require students to cut out number cards, copy the cards on card stock and laminate them to preserve them for future use.

- For activities that include games, provide a homework pass or other prize to the winners.

We hope that the activities in this resource prove to be both interesting and enjoyable for you and your students, and that the activities help your students master the math concepts and skills of the Standards at your grade level. We extend to you our best wishes for a successful and rewarding year.

Judith A. Muschla
Gary Robert Muschla
Erin Muschla-Berry

ABOUT THE AUTHORS

Judith A. Muschla received her BA in mathematics from Douglass College at Rutgers University and is certified to teach K–12. She taught mathematics in South River, New Jersey, for over twenty-five years at various levels at both South River High School and South River Middle School. As a team leader at the middle school, she wrote several math curriculums, coordinated interdisciplinary units, and conducted mathematics workshops for teachers and parents. She also served as a member of the state Review Panel for New Jersey's Mathematics Core Curriculum Content Standards.

Together, Judith and Gary Muschla have coauthored a number of math books published by Jossey-Bass: *Hands-On Math Projects with Real-Life Applications, Grades 3–5* (2009); *The Math Teacher's Problem-a-Day, Grades 4–8* (2008); *Hands-On Math Projects with Real-Life Applications, Grades 6–12* (1996; second edition, 2006); *The Math Teacher's Book of Lists* (1995; second edition, 2005); *Math Games: 180 Reproducible Activities to Motivate, Excite, and Challenge Students, Grades 6–12* (2004); *Algebra Teacher's Activities Kit* (2003); *Math Smart! Over 220 Ready-to-Use Activities to Motivate and Challenge Students, Grades 6–12* (2002); *Geometry Teacher's Activities Kit* (2000); and *Math Starters! 5- to 10-Minute Activities to Make Kids Think, Grades 6–12* (1999).

Gary Robert Muschla received his BA and MAT from Trenton State College and taught in Spotswood, New Jersey, for more than twenty-five years at the elementary school level. He is a successful author and a member of the Authors Guild and the National Writers Association. In addition to math resources, he has written several resources for English and writing teachers; among them are *Writing Workshop Survival Kit* (1993; second edition, 2005); *The Writing Teacher's Book of Lists* (1991; second edition, 2004); *Ready-to-Use Reading Proficiency Lessons and Activities, 10th Grade Level* (2003); *Ready-to-Use Reading Proficiency Lessons and Activities, 8th Grade Level* (2002); *Ready-to-Use Reading Proficiency Lessons and Activities, 4th Grade Level* (2002); *Reading Workshop Survival Kit* (1997); and *English Teacher's Great Books Activities Kit* (1994), all published by Jossey-Bass.

Erin Muschla-Berry received her BS and MEd from The College of New Jersey. She is certified to teach grades K–8 with Mathematics Specialization in grades 5–8. She currently teaches math at Monroe Township Middle School in Monroe, New Jersey, and has presented workshops for math teachers for the Association of Mathematics Teachers of New Jersey. She has coauthored four books with Judith and Gary Muschla for Jossey-Bass: *Math Starters, 2nd Edition: 5- to-10 Minute Activities Aligned with the Common Core Standards, Grades 6–12* (2013); *Teaching the Common Core Math Standards with Hands-On Activities, Grades 6–8* (2012); *The Algebra Teacher's Guide to Reteaching Essential Concepts and Skills* (2011); *The Elementary Teacher's Book of Lists* (2010); and *Math Teacher's Survival Guide, Grades 5–12* (2010).

ACKNOWLEDGMENTS

We thank Jeff Corey Gorman, EdD, assistant superintendent of Monroe Township Public Schools, Chari Chanley, EdS, principal of Monroe Township Middle School, James Higgins, vice principal of Monroe Township Middle School, and Scott Sidler, vice principal of Monroe Township Middle School, for their support.

We also thank Kate Bradford, our editor at Jossey-Bass, for her guidance and suggestions on yet another book.

We want to thank Diane Turso for proofreading this book and putting it into its final form, as she has done with so many others in the past.

We appreciate the support of our many colleagues who, over the years, have encouraged us in our work.

And, of course, we wish to acknowledge the many students we have had the satisfaction of teaching.

CONTENTS

Teaching the Common Core Math Standards with Hands-On Activities, Grades 3–5

Standards and Activities for Grade 3

Operations and Algebraic Thinking: 3.OA.1

"Represent and solve problems involving multiplication and division."

1. "Interpret products of whole numbers, e.g., interpret 5×7 as the total number of objects in 5 groups of 7 objects each."

BACKGROUND

When items in equal-sized groups are combined, multiplication can be used to find the total number of items. For example, hamburger rolls are sold in packages of 8 rolls. If 3 bags are purchased, you can multiply to find the total number of rolls. Three packages (groups) of 8 rolls can be expressed as 3×8. The product is 24 rolls. Note also that $8 \times 3 = 24$, but in this case there are 8 groups of 3 items per group.

 ACTIVITY: COMBINING GROUPS

Working in pairs or groups of three, students will generate ways that groups of items can be represented in real-world situations. They will then draw an illustration of the groups and write a description and a related multiplication sentence.

MATERIALS

Drawing paper; crayons; colored pencils for each pair or group of students.

PROCEDURE

1. Ask your students to think about the ways things are grouped so that each group has the same number of items. Present the example of the hamburger rolls that was provided in the Background section. You may suggest other examples, such as sports (the number of starting players per team), board games (4 cards per person), shopping (6 cupcakes per package), school (5 books per student), and so on. Encourage your students to brainstorm other possible groups.

2. Explain that students are to select an equal-sized group and then decide the number of groups they wish to represent. They are to draw a picture that illustrates their groups. For example, if they chose the packages of hamburger rolls, as noted in the Background section, they would draw 3 packages of hamburger rolls with 8 rolls per package.

3. Explain that after they complete their drawings, they are to write a description of their groups and a multiplication sentence.

CLOSURE

Discuss and display students' drawings, descriptions, and multiplication sentences.

Operations and Algebraic Thinking: 3.OA.2

"Represent and solve problems involving multiplication and division."

2. "Interpret whole-number quotients of whole numbers, e.g., interpret 56 ÷ 8 as the number of objects in each share when 56 objects are partitioned equally into 8 shares, or as a number of shares when 56 objects are partitioned into equal shares of 8 objects each."

BACKGROUND

Division is the process of separating a quantity into equal groups. It is the inverse (opposite) of multiplication, which is the process of combining equal groups.

 ACTIVITY: BREAKING INTO GROUPS

Working in pairs or groups of three, students will find the number of groups that can be formed from a class of 30 students. They will represent their groups on graph paper.

MATERIALS

Two to three sheets of graph paper; 30 counters for each pair or group of students.

PROCEDURE

1. Present this situation to your class: Mr. Smith has a class of 30 students. How many different-sized groups can he form?

2. Explain that because Mr. Smith's class has 30 students, 1 counter represents 1 student.

3. Instruct your students to divide their counters into equal groups to represent the students of Mr. Smith's class. They must find how many groups are possible and then sketch the groups on graph paper. Finally, have students write division sentences that represent their sketches.

CLOSURE

Discuss your students' answers.

ANSWERS

1 group of 30; 2 groups of 15; 3 groups of 10; 5 groups of 6; 6 groups of 5; 10 groups of 3; 15 groups of 2; 30 "groups" of 1

Operations and Algebraic Thinking: 3.OA.3

"Represent and solve problems involving multiplication and division."

3. "Use multiplication and division within 100 to solve word problems in situations involving equal groups, arrays, and measurement quantities, e.g., by using drawings and equations with a symbol for the unknown number to represent the problem."

BACKGROUND

Diagrams and equations may be used with the operations of multiplication and division to solve word problems. Letters are commonly used to represent unknown numbers in equations.

 ACTIVITY: IT'S A MATCH

Working in groups, students will match word problems with equations, diagrams, and answers.

MATERIALS

Scissors; one copy of reproducibles, "Matchings, I" and "Matchings, II," for each group of students.

PROCEDURE

1. Explain that word problems involving multiplication and division can be solved by using equations or diagrams. In equations, symbols may be used to represent unknown numbers. For example, in the problem $3 \times 5 = n$, n represents the product of 3×5, which is 15.

2. Distribute copies of the reproducibles. Explain that together the reproducibles contain 24 boxes that have word problems (boxes 1–8), equations or diagrams (boxes 9–16), and answers (boxes 17–24).

3. Explain that students are to cut out each box.

4. Instruct students to start with problem 1. They should find the equation or diagram that matches the problem. Next they should find the answer that matches the problem. Students should continue in the same manner, matching equations, diagrams, and answers for problems 2, 3, and so on. They should place each set of correct "matchings" in separate piles.

CLOSURE

Discuss students' results.

ANSWERS

The card number of the problem, equation or diagram, and answer are listed in order:
1, 12, 23; 2, 13, 18; 3, 15, 19; 4, 14, 17; 5, 10, 20; 6, 11, 24; 7, 16, 22; 8, 9, 21

1. Mike played video games for 20 hours last week. This was twice as long as he is allowed to play in one week. How long is he allowed to play?	9. $2 \times 24 = n$	17. $n = 5$
2. 24 students in the chorus are to stand on a stage. There are 8 students in a row. How many rows are needed?	10.	18. $n = 3$
3. Sam bought 3 cartons of eggs. Each carton had 12 eggs. How many eggs did he buy?	11.	19. $n = 36$
4. There are 30 desks in a classroom. 6 desks are in each row. How many rows of desks are there?	12. $2 \times n = 20$ and $20 \div 2 = n$	20. $n = 6$

5.	13.	21.
24 students are going on a trip. Parents will be driving them. There is room for 4 students in each car. How many cars are needed?		$n = 48$
6.	14.	22.
Mike's family filled 2 rows of seats in the stadium. Each row has 8 seats. How many of Mike's family attended the game?		$n = 4$
7.	15.	23.
12 cookies are to be placed in 3 boxes. How many cookies are in each box?		$n = 10$
8.	16.	24.
Jane earned $24. A pair of shoes that she wants costs twice what she earned. What is the cost of the shoes?		$n = 16$

Operations and Algebraic Thinking: 3.OA.4

"Represent and solve problems involving multiplication and division."

> 4. "Determine the unknown whole number in a multiplication or division equation relating three whole numbers."

BACKGROUND

To find the missing number in a multiplication or division equation, students should know their basic facts. For example, knowing that $4 \times 3 = 12$ is necessary to find the missing number in equations such as $12 \div ? = 3$ and $12 \div ? = 4$.

ACTIVITY: EQUATION TIC-TAC-TOE

In a twist on the traditional game of tic-tac-toe, students will complete tic-tac-toe boards by randomly choosing and writing nine numbers from 1 to 50 on their boards. After the boards are completed, the teacher presents an equation to the class. If the answer to the equation is on a student's board, the student writes an X over it. The first person who gets three Xs in a row or along a diagonal wins. If no student gets three Xs in a row or along a diagonal, the student who has the most Xs after completing all of the equations is the winner.

MATERIALS

One sheet of unlined paper for each student.

PROCEDURE

1. Explain that students will play equation tic-tac-toe, but note that this is a little different from the standard game of tic-tac-toe. In this game, each student has his or her own board and everyone plays against everyone else at the same time.

2. Distribute the paper. (If you are considering playing more than one round, you might have your students fold their papers in half from top to bottom. Using the front and back of the paper results in four regions, each of which can easily accommodate one tic-tac-toe board. It is likely that you will need to create more equations to play more games.) Instruct your students to draw a tic-tac-toe board on (each region of) their papers as shown.

3. Explain to your students that they are to select any nine numbers from the numbers 1 through 50 and write one number in each space on the tic-tac-toe board. Note that they cannot use any number more than once.

4. Explain that you will present an equation. Students who have the answer on their boards should place an X over the number. There are two ways to win. The first student to get three Xs in a row or along a diagonal wins. If all of the equations have been presented, and no one has three Xs in a row, the student with the most Xs on his or her board is the winner.

5. Begin the game. Present the first equation from the Equation Bank, and continue until someone wins or all of the equations have been used.

CLOSURE

Review the answers after each game to verify the winner. Create equations of your own to play additional games.

Equation Bank

Problem	Answer	Problem	Answer	Problem	Answer
1. $5 \times 5 = ?$	25	11. $? \div 4 = 4$	16	21. $6 \times 4 = ?$	24
2. $8 \times 6 = ?$	48	12. $72 \div 8 = ?$	9	22. $9 \times 5 = ?$	45
3. $? \div 5 = 10$	50	13. $4 \times 7 = ?$	28	23. $? \div 6 = 6$	36
4. $8 \times 4 = ?$	32	14. $? \div 9 = 3$	27	24. $4 \times 5 = ?$	20
5. $? \div 3 = 4$	12	15. $56 \div 7 = ?$	8	25. $? \div 10 = 4$	40
6. $54 \div 9 = ?$	6	16. $16 \div 8 = ?$	2	26. $63 \div 9 = ?$	7
7. $2 \times 9 = ?$	18	17. $3 \times 7 = ?$	21	27. $30 \div 6 = ?$	5
8. $3 \times 10 = ?$	30	18. $36 \div 9 = ?$	4	28. $7 \times 5 = ?$	35
9. $24 \div 8 = ?$	3	19. $2 \times 5 = ?$	10	29. $2 \times 7 = ?$	14
10. $? \div 3 = 5$	15	20. $7 \times 6 = ?$	42	30. $? \div 7 = 7$	49

Operations and Algebraic Thinking: 3.OA.5

"Understand properties of multiplication and the relationship between multiplication and division."

5. "Apply properties of operations as strategies to multiply and divide."

BACKGROUND

Applying mathematical properties can help students compute by changing the order of factors, grouping factors, and expressing a factor as the sum of two numbers.

- The commutative property of multiplication, $a \times b = b \times a$, states that the order of multiplying two factors does not affect their product.

- The associative property of multiplication, $a \times (b \times c) = (a \times b) \times c$, states that the order of grouping factors does not affect their product.

- The distributive property, $a \times (b + c) = a \times b + a \times c$, states that the product of a factor and a sum is equal to multiplying each addend in the sum by the factor and then adding the products.

Although students need not know the names of these properties to complete this activity, an intuitive grasp of the properties will be helpful.

ACTIVITY: APPLYING PROPERTIES

Working in pairs or groups of three, students will apply properties of operations to complete math equations.

MATERIALS

Scissors; one copy of reproducible, "Fact Cards," for each pair or group of students.

PROCEDURE

1. Hand out copies of the reproducible. Explain to your students that the reproducible contains 20 fact cards. Each card is equivalent to 1 of 4 different values.

2. Explain that students are to cut out the cards. They are then to place each card with the other cards that have the same value. (*Note:* They should finish with four sets of cards, though not all sets will have the same number of cards.)

CLOSURE

Check students' results. Ask your students to share strategies they used to arrange their cards correctly. Emphasize that problems can often be solved in different ways.

ANSWERS

Cards that equal 60: 1, 6, 14, 17, 18, and 20.
Cards that equal 40: 2, 7, 9, 15, and 19.
Cards that equal 27: 3, 12, and 16.
Cards that equal 24: 4, 5, 8, 10, 11, and 13.

1. $6 \times (2 \times 5)$	2. 4×10	3. 9×3	4. $2 \times (8 + 4)$
5. 8×3	6. $6 \times (3 + 7)$	7. $(4 \times 2) \times 5$	8. 4×6
9. 8×5	10. $4 \times (5 + 1)$	11. $(3 \times 2) \times 4$	12. $3 \times (7 + 2)$
13. 6×4	14. $6 \times (7 + 3)$	15. $(2 \times 4) \times 5$	16. 3×9
17. $4 \times (8 + 7)$	18. $3 \times (10 + 10)$	19. $4 \times (8 + 2)$	20. 6×10

Operations and Algebraic Thinking: 3.OA.6

"Understand properties of multiplication and the relationship between multiplication and division."

> 6. "Understand division as an unknown-factor problem."

BACKGROUND

Since division and multiplication are inverse operations, every division problem has a related multiplication problem.

For example, $18 \div 3 = ?$ can be posed as "3 times what number is 18?" Students can solve this problem by finding the missing factor of 18. $3 \times ? = 18$ The missing factor is 6.

ACTIVITY: NUMBER SCRAMBLE

Working in pairs or groups of three, students will be given a division problem. They will find the number that completes a multiplication sentence and then find the missing factor.

MATERIALS

Scissors; glue sticks; one copy of reproducibles, "Multiplication, Division, and Factors, I" and "Multiplication, Division, and Factors, II," for each pair or group of students.

PROCEDURE

1. Hand out copies of the reproducibles. Note that "Multiplication, Division, and Factors, I" contains six rows (1 through 6) and that "Multiplication, Division, and Factors, II" contains four rows (7–10). Each row is divided into three parts. The first part contains a division problem. The second part contains a related multiplication sentence that students must complete. The third part contains the answer to the multiplication sentence, which students must provide. Following row 10 is a Number Bank.

2. Explain that students are to cut out the numbers in the Number Bank. They are to glue the correct numbers in the boxes to complete the multiplication sentences. They are also to glue the correct numbers in the boxes for the answers to the multiplication sentences. Note that each multiplication sentence is related to the division problem in its row.

Discuss students' results. While still working in pairs or groups, for more practice, ask your students to write a division problem for their partners. Their partner should then write a related multiplication sentence.

ANSWERS

The missing numbers in each row follow: **(1)** 5, 5, 25; **(2)** 6, 4, 24; **(3)** 3, 2, 6; **(4)** 3, 3, 9; **(5)** 2, 4, 8; **(6)** 8, 5, 40; **(7)** 3, 9, 27; **(8)** 5, 6, 30; **(9)** 8, 3, 24; **(10)** 6, 9, 54

Division	Multiplication Sentence				Answer
1. 25 ÷ 5		times		is	
2. 24 ÷ 6		times		is	
3. 6 ÷ 3		times		is	
4. 9 ÷ 3		times		is	
5. 8 ÷ 2		times		is	
6. 40 ÷ 8		times		is	

Division	Multiplication Sentence				Answer
7. 27 ÷ 3		times		is	
8. 30 ÷ 5		times		is	
9. 24 ÷ 8		times		is	
10. 54 ÷ 6		times		is	

Number Bank					
2	2	3	3	3	3
3	4	4	5	5	5
5	6	6	6	6	8
8	8	9	9	9	24
24	25	27	30	40	54

Operations and Algebraic Thinking: 3.OA.7

"Multiply and divide within 100."

> 7. "Fluently multiply and divide within 100, using strategies such as the relationship between multiplication and division (e.g., knowing that $8 \times 5 = 40$, one knows that $40 \div 5 = 8$) or properties of operations. By the end of Grade 3, know from memory all products of two one-digit numbers."

BACKGROUND

The first step to mastering multiplication and division is to understand how these operations are related. The next step is to be able to multiply and divide quickly and accurately all products of two one-digit numbers. This is achieved through practice and memorization.

ACTIVITY: MULTIPLICATION AND DIVISION BINGO

Students will create a math bingo board by placing numbers from a Number Bank in each square on the board. The teacher will call out multiplication and division problems. If the answer is on the student's board, the student will cover the square with a counter. The first student to cover the squares in a row, column, or diagonal is the winner.

MATERIALS

24 1-inch diameter (or smaller) counters; reproducible, "Multiplication and Division Bingo," for each student. Optional: One copy of reproducible, "Problem Bank for Multiplication and Division Bingo," for the teacher.

PROCEDURE

1. Hand out copies of the bingo boards. Explain that there is a Number Bank below the board.

2. Explain that students should randomly fill in each square on their board with a number from the Number Bank. They should not fill in the free space with a number. As they fill in a number, suggest that they cross out the number in the Number Bank so that they will not use the same number twice. Note that some numbers will not be used.

3. Explain the rules of the game. You will call out a multiplication or division problem from the "Problem Bank for Multiplication and Division Bingo." (*Note:* The answers are written in parentheses after the problems.) Students who find the answer to the problem on their boards should place a counter on the number. (*Note:* Having students use counters to

place on numbers allows you to use the same bingo board for additional games.) After presenting a problem, place a check beside the problems you use on the Problem Bank so that you do not use the problem again. Continue calling out problems until a student gets bingo.

4. Check the answers the student has covered on his bingo board to make sure he is correct.

CLOSURE

Announce the correct answers and review any problems that students found confusing.

		Free Space		

Number Bank

1	2	3	4	5	6	7
8	9	10	12	14	15	16
18	20	21	24	25	27	28
30	32	35	36	40	42	45
48	49	50	54	56	60	63
64	70	72	80	81	90	100

6 × 4 (24)	4 × 8 (32)	9 × 9 (81)
24 ÷ 3 (8)	7 × 6 (42)	60 ÷ 10 (6)
2 × 5 (10)	9 × 10 (90)	6 × 3 (18)
9 × 8 (72)	18 ÷ 9 (2)	8 × 7 (56)
1 × 1 (1)	6 × 9 (54)	10 × 3 (30)
7 × 3 (21)	8 × 5 (40)	9 ÷ 3 (3)
8 × 6 (48)	7 × 7 (49)	6 × 10 (60)
7 ÷ 1 (7)	36 ÷ 4 (9)	6 × 2 (12)
2 × 8 (16)	8 × 8 (64)	5 × 5 (25)
8 ÷ 2 (4)	30 ÷ 6 (5)	7 × 10 (70)
5 × 9 (45)	10 × 10 (100)	6 × 6 (36)
4 × 5 (20)	3 × 5 (15)	9 × 3 (27)
9 × 7 (63)	5 × 10 (50)	7 × 5 (35)
7 × 2 (14)	7 × 4 (28)	8 × 10 (80)

Operations and Algebraic Thinking: 3.OA.8

"Solve problems involving the four operations, and identify and explain patterns in arithmetic."

8. "Solve two-step word problems using the four operations. Represent these problems using equations with a letter standing for the unknown quantity. Assess the reasonableness of answers using mental computation and estimation strategies including rounding."

BACKGROUND

Solving two-step word problems requires several steps:

1. Read the problem carefully.
2. Identify what you are to find.
3. Decide what information to use.
4. Write an equation using a letter to stand for the unknown quantity.
5. Solve the equation.
6. Check to see if your answer makes sense.

ACTIVITY: WHICH EQUATION?

Working in pairs or groups of three, students will choose an equation that can be used to solve word problems. They will then solve the problem.

MATERIALS

Reproducible, "Two-Step Word Problems," for each pair or group of students.

PROCEDURE

1. Review the steps for writing and solving two-step word problems that were presented in the Background of this activity.
2. Hand out copies of the reproducible. Explain that it contains five word problems, each of which is followed by two equations. Students are to select the equation that can be used to solve the problem. They must then solve the problem.
3. Depending on the abilities of your students, you might find it helpful to do the first problem together as a class.

4. Emphasize that after students have selected the correct equation and solved a problem, they must consider whether their answer makes sense by using estimation or mental math. For example, imagine an answer to a problem that the cost of a school lunch is $175. This is unlikely. A probable mistake here is omission of a decimal point that would make a correct (and reasonable) answer of $1.75.

CLOSURE

Discuss the answers to the problems, including students' assessments of the reasonableness of their answers. Ask how they determined if an answer made sense.

ANSWERS

The correct equations are listed, followed by their solution. **(1)** $27 \div 9 + 4 = n$; $n = 7$; **(2)** $5 \times 3 - 14 = n$; $n = 1$; **(3)** $6 \times n = 54 - 12$; $n = 7$ **(4)** $7 \times 4 + 6 = n$; $n = 34$; **(5)** $6 \times 4 - 20 = n$; $n = 4$

TWO-STEP WORD PROBLEMS

Directions: Choose the equation, or equations, that describe each problem. Solve the problem. Decide if your answer is reasonable.

1. Mason has 27 new coins to add to his collection. He will put them in a coin album. Each page holds 9 coins. He already has 4 full pages of coins. After he puts the new coins in his album, how many full pages will he have? n stands for the total number of pages.

$$27 \div 9 = 4 - n \qquad 27 \div 9 + 4 = n$$

2. Mrs. Sanchez plans to hand out markers to 5 groups of students. She wants each group to have 3 markers. She has 14 markers. How many more markers does she need? n stands for the number of additional markers.

$$5 \times 3 - 14 = n \qquad 14 = 5 \times 3 + n$$

3. Audrey is paid $6 a week for walking Ruffles, Mrs. Hanson's dog. Audrey needs $54 to buy her brother a birthday present. She has already earned $12. How many more weeks must she walk Ruffles so that she has enough money to buy the gift? n stands for the number of weeks she must work.

$$54 \div 6 = 12 - n \qquad 6 \times n = 54 - 12$$

4. Sal is decorating 8 cupcakes. He places 6 candies on one of the cupcakes. He places 4 candies on the other 7 cupcakes. How many candies will he need? n stands for the number of candies he needs.

$$4 \times n + 6 = 34 \qquad 7 \times 4 + 6 = n$$

5. Carla is taking 4 packages of soda to a family picnic. Each package has 6 cans. 20 people are at the picnic. Each person drinks one can of soda. How many cans will be left over? n stands for the number of soda cans left over.

$$6 \times 4 - 20 = n \qquad 20 \times 4 + 6 = n$$

Operations and Algebraic Thinking: 3.OA.9

"Solve problems involving the four operations, and identify and explain patterns in arithmetic."

9. "Identify arithmetic patterns (including patterns in the addition table or multiplication table), and explain them using properties of operations."

BACKGROUND

Patterns abound in mathematics. Multiples present students with a variety of patterns. Some are noted below:

- All multiples of 2, 4, 6, 8, and 10 are even.
- Every multiple of 4, 6, 8, and 10 is a multiple of 2.
- Every multiple of 6 and 9 is a multiple of 3.
- Every multiple of 10 is a multiple of 5.

ACTIVITY: COLOR THE MULTIPLES

Students will color the multiples of a number assigned to them on a multiplication table. They will describe a pattern they see and explain it using properties of operations.

MATERIALS

Colored pencils; crayons; reproducible, "Multiplication Table," for each student.

PROCEDURE

1. Assign each student a number from 2 to 10. (More than one student may work with the same number.)

2. Distribute copies of the reproducible. Explain that students who have "2" are to color the multiples of 2 on their multiplication table. Students who have "3" are to color the multiples of 3 on their multiplication table. Other students are to similarly color the multiples of their numbers on the multiplication table.

3. Explain that when students are done coloring their multiples, they are to explain a pattern that they find.

Ask for volunteers to share the numbers they colored. Discuss what patterns they found.
Note any different patterns for the same numbers.

ANSWERS

The patterns students find may vary; some include the following: All multiples of 2 are even numbers. Multiples of 3 may be odd or even. All multiples of 4 are even numbers. All multiples of 5 end in 0 or 5. All multiples of 6 are even numbers. Multiples of 7 may be odd or even. All multiples of 8 are even numbers. Multiples of 9 may be odd or even. All multiples of 10 end in 0.

MULTIPLICATION TABLE

X	1	2	3	4	5	6	7	8	9	10
1	1	2	3	4	5	6	7	8	9	10
2	2	4	6	8	10	12	14	16	18	20
3	3	6	9	12	15	18	21	24	27	30
4	4	8	12	16	20	24	28	32	36	40
5	5	10	15	20	25	30	35	40	45	50
6	6	12	18	24	30	36	42	48	54	60
7	7	14	21	28	35	42	49	56	63	70
8	8	16	24	32	40	48	56	64	72	80
9	9	18	27	36	45	54	63	72	81	90
10	10	20	30	40	50	60	70	80	90	100

Number and Operations in Base Ten: 3.NBT.1

"Use place value understanding and properties of operations to perform multi-digit arithmetic."

1. "Use place value understanding to round whole numbers to the nearest 10 or 100."

BACKGROUND

Rounding is an important skill in mathematics. To round numbers, students must understand place value.

When rounding to the nearest 10, students must look to the digit in the ones place. If the digit is 5 or more, students must round up to the nearest 10. If the digit is 4 or less, they must round down to the nearest 10. For example, 25 is rounded to 30, but 24 is rounded to 20.

When rounding to the nearest 100, students must look to the digit in the tens place. If the digit is 5 or more, they must round up to the nearest 100. If the digit is 4 or less, they must round down to the nearest 100. For example, 855 is rounded to 900, but 845 is rounded to 800.

 ## ACTIVITY: IT'S AROUND ...

Working in pairs or groups of three, students will round numbers to the nearest 10 and nearest 100.

MATERIALS

Reproducible, "Rounding Numbers," for each pair or group of students.

PROCEDURE

1. Distribute copies of the reproducible. Explain that there are two large boxes on the right side of the page. The first contains the numbers 0, 10, 20, 30, 40, 50, and 60. The second contains the numbers 100, 200, 300, 400, 500, 600, and 700. Students will be rounding to these numbers.

2. Explain that the numbers in the box on the upper left of the page are to be used with the numbers in the box immediately to their right. Students are to consider each number in the box on the upper left, and write it beside the number in the box on the right that it can be rounded to. For example, the numbers 49 and 53 (in the box on the upper left) can both be rounded to the number 50 (in the box directly to the right). Students are to write these numbers in the space beside 50 in the box on the right.

3. Explain that the numbers in the box on the lower left of the page are to be used with the numbers in the box immediately to their right. Again, students are to consider each number in the box on the lower left, and write it beside the number in the box on the right that it can be rounded to.

CLOSURE

Correct the work as a class. Review any numbers students had difficulty rounding.

ANSWERS

0: 4; **10:** 5, 7, 11, 14; **20:** 15, 19, 24; **30:** 25, 31; **40:** 35, 44; **50:** 49, 53; **60:** 59, 62; **100:** 79, 120; **200:** 150, 189, 199, 201; **300:** 305, 349; **400:** 370, 410, 449; **500:** 499; **600:** 554, 628; **700:** 705, 745

ROUNDING NUMBERS

Look at each number in the small box below. Write each number in the large box beside the number it can be rounded to.

24	5	53	25
35	44	19	31
59	62	49	4
11	7	14	15

0	
10	
20	
30	
40	
50	
60	

Look at each number in the small box below. Write each number in the large box beside the number it can be rounded to.

120	449	628	189
745	499	150	554
79	199	705	305
349	201	370	410

100	
200	
300	
400	
500	
600	
700	

Number and Operations in Base Ten: 3.NBT.2

"Use place value understanding and properties of operations to perform multi-digit arithmetic."

> 2. "Fluently add and subtract within 1,000 using strategies and algorithms based on place value, properties of operations, and/or the relationship between addition and subtraction."

BACKGROUND

Addition and subtraction problems involving two- and three-digit numbers can be classified in two groups: those problems that do not require regrouping and those that do. You may find it helpful to demonstrate and reinforce the meaning of addition and subtraction, especially the concept of regrouping, through modeling with base-10 blocks.

ACTIVITY 1: HELPING ZERO FIND A PLACE

The teacher will read the story *A Place for Zero: A Math Adventure* to the class. Students are to listen to the story, and then write a letter to Zero, explaining how he is important to the other digits.

MATERIALS

One copy of *A Place for Zero: A Math Adventure* by Angeline Sparagna LoPresti (Charlesbridge Publishing, 2003) for the teacher.

PROCEDURE

1. Read the story *A Place for Zero: A Math Adventure* to your students. The story is about Zero, who feels different from his other digit friends because he believes he has nothing to add.

2. After reading the story, discuss why Zero feels that he is different.

3. Ask your students to imagine that they are a digit, one of Zero's friends. They are to write a letter to Zero, explaining why he is important not only to them but also to addition and subtraction.

CLOSURE

Ask for volunteers to read their letters to Zero. You may also want to display the letters of your students.

ACTIVITY 2: FINDING SUMS AND DIFFERENCES

Students will add or subtract two- and three-digit numbers within 1,000.

MATERIALS

Reproducible, "Problem Grid"; a copy of an appropriate problem group (see Preparation) for each student; scissors; reproducible, "Problem Groups," for the teacher.

PREPARATION

The reproducible, "Problem Groups," is divided into three parts: Group 1, Group 2, and Group 3. Group 1 contains addition and subtraction problems that do not require regrouping. Group 2 contains addition and subtraction problems that require regrouping. Group 3 contains a variety of addition and subtraction problems, some that require regrouping and some that do not. Make a copy of the reproducible, select the skills you want your students to work with, and cut out the appropriate problems, which may be Group 1, Group 2, or Group 3. Make enough copies of this group so that each student will receive a copy.

PROCEDURE

1. Hand out the copies of the "Problem Grid" to your students. Also hand out the copies of the problem group you selected.

2. Explain that each row on the "Problem Grid" has an answer. Following the answer are four blank squares.

3. Explain that students should find each sum or difference on their problem group. They are then to write the problem number and the problem in the square in each row that contains the answer to the problem. Note that different problems will have the same answer. Also note that not all squares on the "Problem Grid" will be filled.

CLOSURE

Review students' results and discuss any problems that your students found troublesome.

ANSWERS

Groups, answers, and problem numbers are provided. Group 1: **241:** 5, 8, 15; **526:** 6, 10, 13; **854:** 3, 4, 7; **371:** 1, 9 12, 14; **604:** 2, 11; Group 2: **241:** 11, 14; **526:** 4, 7, 10, 15; **854:** 1, 9, 12, 13; **371:** 2, 5; **604:** 3, 6, 8; Group 3: **241:** 5, 11, 15; **526:** 2, 4, 8, 13; **854:** 1, 7, 14; **371:** 3, 9; **604:** 6, 10, 12

PROBLEM GRID

Answer	Problems			
241				
526				
854				
371				
604				

PROBLEM GROUPS

Group 1

1. 599 − 228	2. 503 + 101	3. 976 − 122	4. 430 + 424	5. 211 + 30
6. 501 + 25	7. 421 + 433	8. 767 − 526	9. 995 − 624	10. 668 − 142
11. 905 − 301	12. 240 + 131	13. 206 + 320	14. 872 − 501	15. 130 + 111

Group 2

1. 359 + 495	2. 627 − 256	3. 409 + 195	4. 945 − 419	5. 189 + 182
6. 901 − 297	7. 309 + 217	8. 478 + 126	9. 369 + 485	10. 923 − 397
11. 608 − 367	12. 961 − 107	13. 960 − 106	14. 114 + 127	15. 552 − 26

Group 3

1. 343 + 511	2. 114 + 412	3. 209 + 162	4. 804 − 278	5. 328 − 87
6. 909 − 305	7. 981 − 127	8. 404 + 122	9. 486 − 115	10. 206 + 398
11. 567 − 326	12. 299 + 305	13. 923 − 397	14. 976 − 122	15. 118 + 123

Number and Operations in Base Ten: 3.NBT.3

"Use place value understanding and properties of operations to perform multi-digit arithmetic."

> 3. "Multiply one-digit whole numbers by multiples of 10 in the range 10–90 (e.g., 9×80, 5×60) using strategies based on place value and properties of operations."

BACKGROUND

Knowledge of the products of two one-digit numbers makes multiplication of multiples of 10 by one-digit whole numbers a simple process.

For example, 3×20 can easily be found if students know that $3 \times 2 = 6$. They can use a shortcut to find the product by adding a zero in the ones place. Be sure, however, that your students understand why the shortcut can be used. For example, modeling problems such as 3 groups of 20 and finding the sum can help them understand why $3 \times 20 = 60$.

 ACTIVITY: WHAT DOES IT EQUAL?

Students will work individually or in pairs for this activity. They will be given a slip of paper that contains a product and a multiplication problem. They will identify the product, based on the problem.

MATERIALS

One copy of reproducible, "Products and Problems," for the class and one copy for the teacher; scissors for the teacher.

PREPARATION

After making two copies of the reproducible, cut out each two-part box from one copy so that you have a total of 21 slips of paper. (Each student or pair of students will receive one slip.) Keep the other copy of the reproducible to refer to during the activity. Note that the slips are arranged in order, each providing the correct answer to the multiplication problem written on the preceding slip. The first answer, "It equals 80," is the answer to the last problem on the reproducible.

PROCEDURE

1. Before passing out the 21 slips of paper to your students, mix the slips up.

2. Hand out one slip of paper to each student (or a slip to a pair of students). For a small class, you may give some students two slips. You must distribute all 21 slips.

3. To start, choose a student to read the problem written on the right side of his or her slip. If necessary, have the student read the problem twice. All students should check their slips to see if the slips contain the product. Because of the way the slips are designed, only one will contain the correct product. The student who has the slip with the correct product should say "It equals ... " and then provide the answer. If the student is correct, he then reads the question written on the right side of his slip. If he is incorrect, point out his error. Another student should then provide the correct product from the left side of her own slip.

4. Continue the process until the student who read the first question has the correct response to the last question.

CLOSURE

Discuss the activity. Ask your students to explain how knowing the basic multiplication facts helped them multiply whole numbers by multiples of 10.

It equals	What does
80	9 × 40 equal?

It equals	What does
360	3 × 80 equal?

It equals	What does
240	2 × 50 equal?

It equals	What does
100	80 × 4 equal?

It equals	What does
320	2 × 30 equal?

It equals	What does
60	70 × 2 equal?

It equals	What does
140	6 × 50 equal?

It equals	What does
300	9 × 30 equal?

It equals	What does
270	6 × 30 equal?

It equals	What does
180	7 × 60 equal?

It equals	What does
420	5 × 80 equal?

It equals	What does
400	9 × 60 equal?

It equals	What does
540	7 × 90 equal?

It equals	What does
630	6 × 80 equal?

It equals	What does
480	4 × 10 equal?

It equals	What does
40	7 × 80 equal?

It equals	What does
560	5 × 70 equal?

It equals	What does
350	8 × 90 equal?

It equals	What does
720	3 × 40 equal?

It equals	What does
120	7 × 40 equal?

It equals	What does
280	8 × 10 equal?

Number and Operations—Fractions: 3.NF.1

"Develop understanding of fractions as numbers."

> 1. "Understand a fraction $\frac{1}{b}$ as the quantity formed by 1 part when a whole is partitioned into b equal parts; understand a fraction $\frac{a}{b}$ as the quantity formed by a parts of size $\frac{1}{b}$."

BACKGROUND

If a quantity is divided into the same number, n, of equal parts, each part is $\frac{1}{n}$ of the total. For example, if a quantity is divided into 4 equal parts, each part is $\frac{1}{4}$ of the original.

ACTIVITY: MAKING FRACTION BARS

Students will make fraction bars, showing what part each fraction bar is of 1 whole. Because this Domain is limited to fractions with denominators of 2, 3, 4, 6, and 8, students will make fraction bars representing 1, $\frac{1}{2}$, $\frac{1}{3}$, $\frac{1}{4}$, $\frac{1}{6}$, and $\frac{1}{8}$.

MATERIALS

Scissors; rulers; unlined $8\frac{1}{2}$-by-11-inch paper for each student.

PROCEDURE

1. Explain to your students that they are to cut six 1-inch-by-10-inch strips of paper from their unlined paper. (Demonstrate what students should do.) A practical way to do this is to cut off a 1-inch-by-$8\frac{1}{2}$-inch strip from the top of the paper, leaving an $8\frac{1}{2}$-inch-by-10-inch piece of paper. Next, students should cut a $2\frac{1}{2}$-inch-by-10-inch strip off one of the sides of the paper, leaving a 6-inch-by-10-inch piece of paper. Students should discard the strips of paper they cut off. (*Note:* Depending on the abilities of your students, you may prefer to use a paper cutter and hand out precut 6-inch-by-10-inch sheets and then allow students to cut the paper into the necessary strips.)

2. Instruct your students to place their paper so that it measures 10 inches along the top and 6 inches along the side. They should mark points at 1-inch intervals along each side, and then draw lines connecting each pair of points. Next they should cut along each line, resulting in six 1-inch-by-10-inch strips.

3. Tell your students to label one strip *1 whole*.

4. Instruct them to take another strip. They should fold it in half, open the strip, and then write $\frac{1}{2}$ on each part of the strip.

5. Instruct your students to take another strip. They should fold this strip in half, then fold it in half again. After opening the strip, they should label each part $\frac{1}{4}$.

6. Instruct your students to take another strip. They should fold this strip in half, fold it in half again, and fold it in half once more. After opening the strip, they should label each part $\frac{1}{8}$.

7. Instruct them to take another strip. They are to fold this strip in thirds. After opening the strip, they should label each part $\frac{1}{3}$.

8. Instruct your students to take the final strip. They are to fold this strip in thirds, then fold it in half. After opening the strip, they should label each part $\frac{1}{6}$.

9. Using these strips, ask your students questions such as the following:

- What strips represent $\frac{2}{3}$? (Answer: Two parts of the $\frac{1}{3}$ strip or four parts of the $\frac{1}{6}$ strip)

- What strips represent $\frac{1}{4}$? (Answer: One part of the $\frac{1}{4}$ strip or two parts of the $\frac{1}{8}$ strip)

- What strips represent 1 whole? (Answer: Two $\frac{1}{2}$, three $\frac{1}{3}$, four $\frac{1}{4}$, six $\frac{1}{6}$, or eight $\frac{1}{8}$ parts or one *1 whole* strip)

CLOSURE

Ask your students to explain how fraction bars help them to understand fractions.

Number and Operations — Fractions: 3.NF.2

"Develop understanding of fractions as numbers."

2. "Understand a fraction as a number on the number line; represent fractions on a number line diagram.

  a. "Represent a fraction $\frac{1}{b}$ on a number line diagram by defining the interval from 0 to 1 as the whole and partitioning it into b equal parts. Recognize that each part has size $\frac{1}{b}$ and that the endpoint of the part based at 0 locates the number $\frac{1}{b}$ on the number line.

  b. "Represent a fraction $\frac{a}{b}$ on a number line diagram by marking off a lengths $\frac{1}{b}$ from 0. Recognize that the resulting interval has size $\frac{a}{b}$ and that its endpoint locates the number $\frac{a}{b}$ on the number line."

BACKGROUND

Every fraction can be represented on a number line by marking off equal parts (represented by the denominator of the fraction) and counting off the number of equal parts (represented by the numerator of the fraction).

For example, to locate $\frac{3}{4}$ on a number line, divide the portion of the number line from 0 to 1 into 4 equal intervals. Then, from 0, count 3 of these intervals and place a dot on the line. Note that the fourth interval is $\frac{4}{4}$, which is the same as 1.

ACTIVITY: PLACING FRACTIONS ON THE NUMBER LINE

Working at a Web site, students will move a cursor along a virtual number line to represent fractions.

MATERIALS

Computers with Internet access for students; computer and digital projector for the teacher.

PROCEDURE

1. Instruct your students to go to www.mathisfun.com/numbers/fraction-number-line.html where they will find a virtual number line that ranges from 0 to 1.

2. Demonstrate how students can locate fractions on the number line. Start at 0 and move the cursor along the number line at the top, stopping at 1 whole. The values of fractions will be displayed. Point out the intervals on the number line and how they correspond

to the values of the fractions. Note that the vertical line that highlights the fraction also highlights equivalent fractions.

3. Instruct your students to locate $\frac{1}{4}, \frac{1}{2}, \frac{4}{6}$, and $\frac{7}{8}$ on the number line. Give them a chance to locate the fractions, then locate them yourself so that students can see if they are correct.

CLOSURE

Discuss the activity. Ask questions such as the following: What other values are the same as $\frac{1}{2}$? $\left(\text{Answer: } \frac{2}{4}, \frac{3}{6}, \frac{4}{8}\right)$ What other values are the same as $\frac{4}{6}$? $\left(\text{Answer: } \frac{2}{3}\right)$ (*Note:* The previous answers are limited to halves, thirds, fourths, sixths, and eighths, which are the focus of fractions in third grade.) Students should realize that fractions and their equivalent values can be located on the number line.

Number and Operations—Fractions: 3.NF.3

"Develop understanding of fractions as numbers."

3. "Explain equivalence of fractions in special cases, and compare fractions by reasoning about their size.

  a. "Understand two fractions as equivalent (equal) if they are the same size, or the same point on a number line.

  b. "Recognize and generate simple equivalent fractions, e.g., $\frac{1}{2} = \frac{2}{4}, \frac{4}{6} = \frac{2}{3}$. Explain why the fractions are equivalent, e.g., by using a visual fraction model.

  c. "Express whole numbers as fractions, and recognize fractions that are equivalent to whole numbers.

  d. "Compare two fractions with the same numerator or the same denominator by reasoning about their size. Recognize that comparisons are valid only when the two fractions refer to the same whole. Record the results of comparisons with the symbols >, =, or <, and justify the conclusions, e.g., by using a visual fraction model."

BACKGROUND

Fractions may be expressed in many forms. Two common forms are equivalent fractions (fractions that have the same value) and whole numbers (which can be written as a fraction with 1 as the denominator).

If two fractions have the same numerator, the fraction that has the larger denominator has the smaller value. For example, $\frac{1}{3}$ is less than $\frac{1}{2}$. Given two pies of equal size, cut one into thirds and the other into halves. It is clear that a piece that is $\frac{1}{3}$ of the original pie is smaller than a piece that is $\frac{1}{2}$ of the original pie.

If two fractions have the same denominator and different numerators, the fraction with the larger numerator has the larger value. The fraction with the larger numerator represents more of the equal parts. For example, $\frac{7}{8}$ has a greater value than $\frac{5}{8}$, because 7 parts, each part being $\frac{1}{8}$, are larger than 5 parts, each being $\frac{1}{8}$.

 ACTIVITY 1: SQUARES AND FRACTIONS

Working in pairs or groups of three, students will cut out four squares and arrange them so that equivalent values correspond to form a large square.

MATERIALS

Scissors; reproducible, "Four Squares," for each pair or group of students.

PROCEDURE

1. Review equivalent fractions and whole numbers expressed as fractions. For example, $\frac{1}{2} = \frac{2}{4}$ and $3 = \frac{3}{1}$.

2. Hand out copies of the reproducible and explain that students will see four squares, each of which contains fractions and a whole number.

3. Instruct your students to cut out each square.

4. Explain that they should arrange the squares so that the sides that have equivalent fractions are next to each other. Note that the numbers on the squares may not be turned upside down. Remind students that whole numbers may be written as fractions.

CLOSURE

Discuss the positions of the squares with your students.

ANSWERS

Two possible arrangements are shown below.

Arrangement 1 (left):

Top-left square: top $\frac{2}{1}$, left 4, right $\frac{2}{4}$, bottom $\frac{1}{4}$.
Top-right square: top 2, left $\frac{1}{2}$, right $\frac{4}{1}$, bottom $\frac{1}{3}$.
Bottom-left square: top $\frac{2}{8}$, left 3, right $\frac{4}{6}$, bottom $\frac{5}{1}$.
Bottom-right square: top $\frac{2}{6}$, left $\frac{2}{3}$, right $\frac{3}{1}$, bottom 5.

Arrangement 2 (right):

Top-left square: top 2, left $\frac{1}{2}$, right $\frac{4}{1}$, bottom $\frac{1}{3}$.
Top-right square: top $\frac{2}{1}$, left 4, right $\frac{2}{4}$, bottom $\frac{1}{4}$.
Bottom-left square: top $\frac{2}{6}$, left $\frac{2}{3}$, right $\frac{3}{1}$, bottom 5.
Bottom-right square: top $\frac{2}{8}$, left 3, right $\frac{4}{6}$, bottom $\frac{5}{1}$.

ACTIVITY 2: BALANCING FRACTIONS

Working at a Web site, students will virtually drag fraction bars to a scale to determine their relative size.

MATERIALS

Computers with Internet access for students; computer and digital projector for the teacher.

PROCEDURE

1. Instruct your students to go to http://mathplayground.com/Scale_Fractions.html. Explain that they will use a virtual balance scale to compare fractions.

2. Demonstrate how to compare fractions using the virtual balance. For example, drag $\frac{1}{2}$ to the left side of the scale and $\frac{1}{3}$ to the right. The ">" is displayed on the scale because $\frac{1}{2} > \frac{1}{3}$. Next, click "Reset." Drag five $\frac{1}{8}$ pieces to the left side of the scale and seven $\frac{1}{8}$ pieces to the right side to show that $\frac{5}{8} < \frac{7}{8}$.

3. Instruct your students to drag other fractions to the scale and write at least five comparisons. They should record their comparisons so that they can share their results with the class at the conclusion of the activity.

CLOSURE

Discuss the comparisons that students made. Discuss any patterns students noticed. For example, they should notice that when the denominators are the same, the larger numerator represents the larger fraction.

$$\frac{2}{1}$$

4 $\qquad$ $\frac{2}{4}$

$$\frac{1}{4}$$

$$\frac{2}{6}$$

$\frac{2}{3}$ $\qquad$ $\frac{3}{1}$

5

$$\frac{2}{8}$$

3 $\qquad$ $\frac{4}{6}$

$$\frac{5}{1}$$

2

$\frac{1}{2}$ $\qquad$ $\frac{4}{1}$

$$\frac{1}{3}$$

Measurement and Data: 3.MD.1

"Solve problems involving measurement and estimation of intervals of time, liquid volumes, and masses of objects."

1. "Tell and write time to the nearest minute and measure time intervals in minutes. Solve word problems involving addition and subtraction of time intervals in minutes, e.g., by representing the problem on a number line diagram."

BACKGROUND

Telling time is an essential skill. By looking at a circular clock students can tell what time it is, what time it will be later, or what time it was a few moments ago. For example, if it is 2:15, students may count by fives to find the time in 20 minutes—2:20, 2:25, 2:30, 2:35.

ACTIVITY 1: TIME TO READ

You will read *Telling Time with Big Mama Cat* by Dan Harper to your class. Students will determine what the time is as you read about the events in the story.

MATERIALS

A copy of the book *Telling Time with Big Mama Cat* by Dan Harper (HMH Books, 1998) for the teacher.

PROCEDURE

1. Explain that you will read a story about Big Mama Cat and time. Start by showing the fold-out clock at the front of the book. Adjust the hands so that they coincide with the start of the story.

2. Read aloud. Pause as you say a time and then show the time on the clock.

3. Ask your students questions at different points in the story. For example: What time is it now?

4. Continue this procedure until you are finished reading.

CLOSURE

Note the actual time in class. Ask students: What time will it be in 10 minutes? 15 minutes? 20 minutes? 30 minutes? 45 minutes? 1 hour and a half? Include more examples if you feel it is necessary.

ACTIVITY 2: WHAT TIME IS IT?

Working at a Web site, students will find the correct time on virtual clocks.

MATERIALS

Computers with Internet access for students; computer and digital project for the teacher.

PROCEDURE

1. Instruct your students to go to http://nlvm.usu.edu/en/. They should click in the grades "3–5" column on the "Measurement" row and then scroll down and click on "Time—What Time Will It Be?" Explain that students will see two clocks and a question regarding time. The clocks have the same time. Students are to answer the question by changing the time on the second clock. (*Note:* The clocks will be either analog or digital and will randomly change with new problems.)

2. Explain that they should show the new time on the round clock by moving the hands on the second clock, or on the digital clock by clicking on the arrows below the second clock. Demonstrate how to increase or decrease the time on the clocks.

3. Explain that after students have changed the time on the second clock, they should click on "Check Answer" to see if they are right. If they are, they should click on "New Problem." If they are wrong, they should try again to find the correct time.

4. Instruct students to try several problems on their own.

CLOSURE

Ask additional questions for which students must find the correct time. For example: If a movie starts at 7:15, and you are 10 minutes late, what time did you arrive at the theater? If it is 12:35, and you have a music lesson in 45 minutes, what time is your lesson?

Measurement and Data: 3.MD.2

"Solve problems involving measurement and estimation of intervals of time, liquid volumes, and masses of objects."

> 2. "Measure and estimate liquid volumes and masses of objects, using standard units of grams (g), kilograms (kg), and liters (L). Add, subtract, multiply, or divide to solve one-step word problems involving masses or volumes that are given in the same units, e.g., by using drawings (such as a beaker with a measurement scale) to represent the problem."

BACKGROUND

Common units of the metric system are grams (g) and kilograms (kg) for measuring mass, which is the amount of matter in an object, and liters (L) for measuring capacity, which is the amount a container can hold. Following are some general descriptions:

- A gram is a very small mass, about 0.035 ounce. Objects such as a paper clip or thumbtack weigh about 1 gram.

- A kilogram is equal to 1,000 grams, about 2.2 pounds. A typical textbook or a pair of sneakers weighs about a kilogram.

- A liter is equal to 1,000 milliliters, about 1.06 quarts. A glass of water is about $\frac{1}{4}$ of a liter. A common type of soda bottle contains 1 liter of soda.

 ACTIVITY 1: MAKE A METRIC MONSTER

This is likely to be a two- or three-day activity. Working in groups of three or four, students will create a metric monster (figure) from common items found in the classroom or at home.

MATERIALS

A metric scale; glue sticks; scissors; construction paper; items such as boxes (for example, empty cereal boxes), cylinders (empty paper towel rolls), circles (paper plates), and also pencils, erasers, notecards, spools of threads—any items that students can estimate and weigh; reproducible, "Recording the Metric Monster Mass," for each group of students; digital camera for the teacher to photograph the metric monsters.

PREPARATION

In the days before the actual activity, encourage students to bring items from home that they will use to build their metric monsters; you may also collect a variety of items ahead of time.

(*Note:* Items should be nonbreakable, safe, and easy to manage in the classroom; for example, discourage students from bringing in glass containers.)

PROCEDURE

Day 1

1. Explain the activity to your students: They will be creating a Metric Monster out of common materials.

2. Encourage them to brainstorm what kinds of items they might use to create their Metric Monster. Students should then decide what items they need and what items each student will bring to class. (*Note:* You may want to give students a few days to bring items into class before moving on to Day 2 of the activity.)

Day 2

1. Explain that kilograms and grams are units of measurement used for measuring mass in the metric system. Mass is the amount of matter in an object. Ask your students if they can name some objects that might be measured in kilograms and grams. Offer some examples, such as those provided in the Background.

2. Hand out copies of the reproducible and explain that it contains spaces to record each item students use in making their Metric Monster. It also contains spaces for the estimated mass of each item, the actual mass of each item, and the difference between them.

3. Make sure that students have enough materials. If necessary, provide some that you brought to class.

4. Instruct students to record the name of each item they use for their Metric Monster in the first column on the reproducible. They are to estimate the weight of each item in grams or kilograms and record the estimated mass in the second column. Next they should weigh each item and record its actual mass in the third column. Finally, they are to find the difference in the values of the estimated and actual mass and record the difference in the fourth column.

5. Encourage students to create their Metric Monsters. Take pictures of their monsters and print them. (*Note:* Be sure to follow the guidelines of your school for taking pictures in class.)

Day 3

1. Distribute the pictures of students' Metric Monsters.

2. Instruct students to attach the pictures to their sheet, "Recording the Metric Monster Mass."

CLOSURE

Discuss the mass of your students' monsters. Ask questions such as the following: How did your estimates of the mass of various items compare to the actual mass of the items? Did the accuracy of your estimates improve as you found the actual mass? Why might this have been? Which monster had the greatest mass? Which had the least? How does the mass of the Metric Monster of one group compare to the mass of another group's Metric Monster? Display the "Recording the Metric Monster Mass" sheets and photos.

ACTIVITY 2: A LOT OF WATER

The teacher presents five containers partially filled with water to the class. Students will estimate the amount of water in each container. The teacher and student volunteers will verify the results by finding the capacity. Students will then write and solve word problems based on the results.

MATERIALS

Unlined paper for each student; a dark nonpermanent marker; five clear containers of various shapes and sizes, such as a milk container, water bottle, soda bottle, vase, and glass; three 1-liter beakers for the teacher.

PREPARATION

Label the containers 1 through 5 with the nonpermanent marker. Use the marker to draw a line on each container to indicate the amount of water you will pour into the container. Then fill each container to the line.

PROCEDURE

1. Explain that liters are the basic unit for measuring capacity in the metric system. Capacity is the amount a container can hold. Ask your students if they can name some items that might be measured in liters. Offer some examples, such as those provided in the Background.

2. Explain to your students that you have five containers filled with water.

3. Ask students to decide how much water, in liters, is in each container. On their sheet of unlined paper, they should sketch each container with its water level so that they have a representation of its contents. They should then record their estimates for container 1, container 2, and so on beneath their sketches.

4. After your students have recorded their estimates, find the capacity of container 1 by pouring the contents into the liter beakers. Have a student volunteer come up, read the volume, and write the amount on the board, along with the container number.

5. Ask your students to compare their estimates with the actual measurement. They should write the actual measurement next to their estimate.

6. Empty the beaker either by pouring the contents into a sink or back into its original container.

7. Follow this same procedure (Steps 3 to 5) for the next four containers.

8. Instruct your students to refer to their sketches, estimates, and the actual measurements, and write a one-step word problem involving either addition, subtraction, multiplication, or division.

CLOSURE

Ask your students how their estimates compared to the actual measurements. Who was closest? Ask for volunteers to share their problems with the class so that other students may solve the problems. Discuss the problems and their answers.

Name _____ Date _____

RECORDING THE METRIC MONSTER MASS

Item	Estimated Mass	Actual Mass	Difference
1.			
2.			
3.			
4.			
5.			
6.			
7.			
8.			
9.			
10.			

Total Mass _____

Measurement and Data: 3.MD.3

"Represent and interpret data."

> 3. "Draw a scaled picture graph and a scaled bar graph to represent a data set with several categories. Solve one- and two-step 'how many more' and 'how many less' problems using information presented in scaled bar graphs."

BACKGROUND

Picture graphs and bar graphs are two very common methods of displaying data. A picture graph is a graph that uses pictures or symbols to display data. A bar graph is a graph that uses horizontal or vertical bars to display data.

 ACTIVITY: PICTURE GRAPHS AND BAR GRAPHS

This activity begins with the teacher gathering data by conducting a poll of the class. Working in pairs or groups of three, students will create scaled picture graphs and bar graphs to represent the data. They will also solve problems based on the graphs.

MATERIALS

Unlined white paper; rulers; markers; crayons; colored pencils for each pair or group of students.

PREPARATION

Conduct a poll of favorites of your students. You might ask students what their favorite flavor of ice cream is (for example, chocolate, vanilla, strawberry, cherry, other); their favorite sport (baseball, football, soccer, basketball, hockey, other); their favorite type of school lunch (pizza, hamburger, hot dog, taco, pasta, other). Of course, you may choose other topics, but whichever topic you choose, limit the possible choices to 5 or 6.

PROCEDURE

1. Conduct the poll and write the data on the board.

2. Explain that picture graphs display data as pictures or symbols. Each picture or symbol represents a specific quantity, which is shown in a legend on the graph. Show your students examples of picture graphs in their math or other texts. You may also find many examples online by searching for "picture graphs." Discuss the graphs and point out how they are constructed.

3. Explain that a bar graph displays data using vertical or horizontal bars. The scale of a bar graph typically represents numerical data. Note that the data is labeled and the bars are separated by a space. Show your students examples of bar graphs in their math or other texts. You may also find many examples online by searching for "bar graphs." Discuss the graphs and point out how they are constructed.

4. Instruct your students to construct a picture graph and a bar graph, using the data obtained in the poll you conducted at the beginning of the activity. Suggest that they choose a simple picture to represent data for their picture graph and create a legend showing the value of each picture. For their bar graph they should create a scale to represent the data, and be sure to label each bar. They should construct their graphs neatly and accurately, and include a title for each graph.

5. After students have constructed their graphs, ask them questions based on comparisons of the data, especially questions that focus on "how many more," and "how much less."

CLOSURE

Ask your students to summarize the steps for constructing picture graphs and bar graphs:

- Obtain data.
- Determine a scale or legend, depending on the graph.
- Draw the graph.
- Show and label the data accurately.
- Include a scale or legend that shows the value of the data on the graph.
- Title the graph.

You may also want to display students' graphs.

Measurement and Data: 3.MD.4

"Represent and interpret data."

4. "Generate measurement data by measuring lengths using rulers marked with halves and fourths of an inch. Show the data by making a line plot, where the horizontal scale is marked off in appropriate units—whole numbers, halves, or quarters."

BACKGROUND

A line plot, also known as a dot plot, displays data along a number line. Each value of the data is marked with a symbol noting the frequency.

For example, suppose that you wish to draw a line plot, showing the hand span of five students in inches: $5\frac{1}{4}$, $5\frac{1}{2}$, 5, 5, 6. The line plot appears below.

Hand Spans

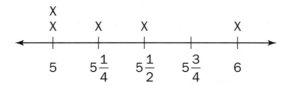

Note that an "X" is placed above the value each time the value appears.

🏃 ACTIVITY: HAND SPANS

Working in pairs or groups of three, students will measure their hand spans and draw a line plot that shows the hand spans of the students in class.

MATERIALS

Rulers with a $\frac{1}{4}$-inch scale; reproducible, "Hand Span Data Sheet," for each pair or group of students.

PROCEDURE

1. Explain that students will measure their hand span—the distance between the tip of the pinkie finger and the tip of the thumb when the hand is open, palm down.

2. Demonstrate a hand span by placing your hand palm down on the board, marking the tip of your pinkie and the tip of your thumb. Then measure the distance between these two points to the nearest quarter inch.

3. Instruct your students to find their hand span and record its length to the nearest quarter inch. If necessary, the student's partner can help measure.

4. Distribute copies of the reproducible. Note that it contains a table (broken into three parts) with rows numbered 1–30 and a horizontal line at the bottom that will serve as the line plot.

5. Call the name of the first student in your grade book. Ask for his or her hand span. Students will record this distance in Row 1 on the reproducible. You may find it helpful to write the data on the board.

6. Continue until all the names of your students have been called and everyone has announced his or her hand span. The number of completed rows in the table should be the same as the number of students in class.

7. Explain how to construct the line plot.

   - Find the smallest and largest hand spans.

   - Place a small vertical line near the left arrow on the horizontal line at the bottom of the reproducible to represent the smallest hand span.

   - Using a ruler and starting with the smallest value, mark the number line at $\frac{1}{4}$-inch intervals, stopping at the number representing the largest hand span.

   - Place an X every time a value is given.

CLOSURE

Discuss the line plots. Ask your students question such as: What was the most common hand span in the class? What was the least common? Is a line plot a good tool for displaying data? Why?

HAND SPAN DATA SHEET

Student	Hand Span
1	
2	
3	
4	
5	
6	
7	
8	
9	
10	

Student	Hand Span
11	
12	
13	
14	
15	
16	
17	
18	
19	
20	

Student	Hand Span
21	
22	
23	
24	
25	
26	
27	
28	
29	
30	

Hand Spans

Measurement and Data: 3.MD.5

"Geometric measurement: understand concepts of area and relate area to multiplication and to addition."

5. "Recognize area as an attribute of plane figures and understand concepts of area measurement.

  a. "A square with side length 1 unit, called 'a unit square,' is said to have 'one square unit' of area, and can be used to measure area.

  b. "A plane figure which can be covered without gaps or overlaps by n unit squares is said to have an area of n square units."

BACKGROUND

The area of plane figures can be measured by covering the figure with square units. Covering a plane figure with square units can help students recognize area.

 ACTIVITY: COVERING THE AREA

Working in groups, students will cover a 1-foot square with 1-inch square tiles.

MATERIALS

About 150 1-inch square tiles; large construction paper (12 inches by 18 inches); rulers with a 1-inch scale; scissors for each group of students.

PROCEDURE

1. Explain that area is the number of square units needed to cover a surface. For this activity students will cover a surface with square units to find the area of the surface.

2. Instruct your students to use their rulers to accurately measure a square with sides of 1 foot (12 inches) on their paper. If they are using paper that is 12 inches by 18 inches, they can do this by taking the paper lengthwise and measuring 6 inches along one side. Tell them to mark a point 6 inches from the short edge at the top of the sheet and a point 6 inches from the short edge at the bottom. Drawing a straight line connecting these two points should result in a 1-foot square on their paper. Demonstrate how they should do this.

3. After students have drawn their square, instruct them to cut along the line that they drew. They should now have a 1-foot square.

4. Explain that they are now to use their 1-inch square tiles to cover the area of their 1-foot square. Each tile should be placed so that its edges neatly fit against the other tiles around it. The tiles should completely cover the 1-foot square without leaving any gaps or overlaps.

CLOSURE

Discuss your students' covered squares. How many 1-inch squares were required to cover the 1-foot square? Emphasize that the 1-foot square is covered with 144 1-inch squares, meaning it has an area of 144 square inches.

Measurement and Data: 3.MD.6

"Geometric measurement: understand concepts of area and relate area to multiplication and to addition."

> 6. "Measure areas by counting unit squares (square cm, square m, square in, square ft, and improvised units.)"

BACKGROUND

The area of a plane figure can easily be measured by counting square units. The number of square units equals the area of the figure.

ACTIVITY 1: MEASURING AREAS

Students will measure the area of flat surfaces by counting unit squares.

MATERIALS

Scissors; rulers with centimeter and inch units; reproducibles, "5-Inch Square" and "10-Centimeter Square," for each student.

PROCEDURE

1. Hand out copies of the reproducibles. Explain that students are to cut out the 5-inch square and 10-centimeter square.

2. Explain that they are to measure each square with their rulers and decide how the surface of the paper can be divided into square units.

3. Explain that after students have determined what square units each large square can be divided into, they should use rulers to draw square units on the paper. Next they should count the total number of square units needed to cover the surface of each square without any gaps or overlaps.

CLOSURE

Discuss students' results. The square with sides of 5 inches can be divided into 1-inch square units and has an area of 25 square units. The square with sides of 10 centimeters can be divided into 1-centimeter square units and has an area of 100 square centimeters.

ACTIVITY 2: MEASURING AREAS WITH APPROPRIATE TOOLS

Working in small groups, students will measure areas with unit squares.

MATERIALS

Meter sticks; yard sticks; 1-foot rulers with inch and centimeter scales for each group; masking tape for the teacher.

PREPARATION

Before students enter the classroom, measure various rectangles and squares on the classroom floor and mark the corners of the figures with masking tape, for example a 2-meter-by-1-meter rectangle, a 2-yard square, and a 4-foot square. Also designate the surfaces of various objects such as desks, tables, bulletin boards, books, windowsills, and the door to the classroom for measurement. Be sure to find the areas of these figures prior to the activity.

PROCEDURE

1. Explain to your students that they will be using meter sticks, yard sticks, and rulers to find the areas of various figures. Remind them that areas are measured in square units.

2. Show your students the figures that they will be measuring. Tell them that they will need to use the appropriate tool—a meter stick, yard stick, or ruler (in inches or centimeters)—to find as closely as possible the number of unit squares that will cover each particular figure, without any gaps or overlaps.

3. Instruct groups to designate a recorder who will write down the number of square units needed to cover each figure.

4. To avoid congestion and idle "waiting around," have groups work at different parts of the classroom, measuring different figures.

5. Remind students that they should try to be as accurate as possible in measuring and then counting the number of unit squares they find in each figure.

CLOSURE

Discuss your students' results. Which group's results were closest to the actual area of each figure? What, if any, problems did students have in measuring the figures? How did they resolve the problems? Emphasize that the area of a plane figure can always be found by counting the unit squares that cover the area completely.

Measurement and Data: 3.MD.7

"Geometric measurement: understand concepts of area and relate area to multiplication and to addition."

7. "Relate area to the operations of multiplication and addition.

   a. "Find the area of a rectangle with whole-number side lengths by tiling it, and show that the area is the same as would be found by multiplying the side lengths.

   b. "Multiply side lengths to find areas of rectangles with whole-number side lengths in the context of solving real-world and mathematical problems, and represent whole-number products as rectangular areas in mathematical reasoning.

   c. "Use tiling to show in a concrete case that the area of a rectangle with whole-number side lengths a and $b + c$ is the sum of $a \times b$ and $a \times c$. Use area models to represent the distributive property in mathematical reasoning.

   d. "Recognize area as additive. Find areas of rectilinear figures by decomposing them into nonoverlapping rectangles and adding the areas of the nonoverlapping parts, applying this technique to solve real-world problems."

BACKGROUND

The area of a rectangle can be found by counting the number of tiles that cover it with no part of the tiles overlapping. Think of a rectangle as being a grid, consisting of rows and columns.

In the example below, because the rectangle has 3 rows with 4 squares in each row, the area is 3×4 or 12 square units.

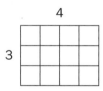

The way to express the area of a rectangle can vary. The rectangle above may be decomposed into two rectangles as pictured below. The 4 columns can be redrawn as $1 + 3$, resulting in a 1-by-3 rectangle and a 3-by-3 rectangle. (*Note:* To avoid confusion with terminology, a square is a special type of rectangle.)

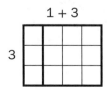

The area of the previous rectangle can be found by using the distributive property: $3 \times (1 + 3) = 3 \times 1 + 3 \times 3$. The sum of nonoverlapping parts can be used to find the total area, showing that area is additive.

 ## ACTIVITY 1: TILING AND FINDING AREA

Students will tile a 3-inch-by-5-inch index card, and then find the area by multiplying the lengths of its sides. They will solve a real-world problem by multiplying the sides of a rectangle to find area.

MATERIALS

One 3-inch-by-5-inch index card; about 20 1-inch square color tiles for each student.

PROCEDURE

1. Explain that students will find the area of an index card by tiling (covering it with 1-inch squares).

2. Explain that students should cover the index card with the 1-inch squares completely, without leaving any gaps or having overlapping squares. After they have completed their tiling, ask: How many 1-inch squares were needed to cover the index card? (Students should have found 15.) Note that this is the area of the index card.

3. Tell your students to find the area of the index card by multiplying its length times its width. $A = l \times w$ ($A = 5 \times 3 = 15$ square inches)

4. Ask your students to compare the areas by tiling and multiplying. (Both are 15 square inches.)

5. Now pose this problem: Mrs. Williams is planning to change her kitchen floor. She needs to buy 1-foot square tiles to cover the floor, which is 9 feet by 10 feet. What is the area of the floor? (90 square feet) How many tiles does she need? (90)

CLOSURE

Ask your students questions such as the following: Does multiplying the length times the width of a rectangle always result in the area of a rectangle? (Students should realize this is true, because the width represents the number of rows, and the length represents the number of squares in each row. The product shows the number of squares needed to tile the rectangle, which is the number of square units.) Is finding the area of a rectangle by multiplying its length by its width easier than counting tiles? Ask your students to explain their answers.

ACTIVITY 2: DECOMPOSING AREAS

Working in pairs or groups of three, students will decompose area models to represent the distributive property.

MATERIALS

Graph paper; reproducible, "The Area of the Sums," for each pair or group of students.

PROCEDURE

1. Explain that rectangles can be decomposed (separated) into smaller rectangles. The area of the original rectangle is equal to the sum of the areas of smaller rectangles.

2. Distribute copies of the reproducible. Explain that at the top is a rectangle whose area is 6 square units. Below it are two different ways to decompose the rectangle into two smaller rectangles. (*Note:* If students point out that in the first example the original rectangle is decomposed into a rectangle and a square, remind them that a square is a special type of rectangle.)

3. Instruct your students to draw a rectangle that has two rows, each with five squares, on their graph paper.

4. Instruct them to decompose this rectangle into two smaller rectangles and find the area of each pair. There are three ways to do this. They should find all three.

CLOSURE

Discuss the ways the rectangle can be decomposed. Ask your students: Do you think the sum of the areas of the smaller rectangles will always equal the area of the original rectangle? Why?

ANSWERS

There are three ways to decompose the rectangle: a 2-by-1 and a 2-by-4 rectangle; a 2-by-2 and a 2-by-3 rectangle; a pair of 1-by-5 rectangles.

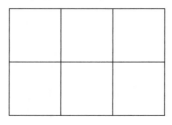

6 Square Units

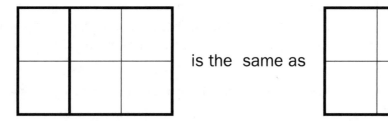

is the same as

2 Square Units + 4 Square Units   4 Square Units + 2 Square Units

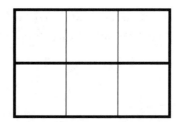

3 Square Units + 3 Square Units

Measurement and Data: 3.MD.8

"Geometric measurement: recognize perimeter as an attribute of plane figures and distinguish between linear and area measures."

8. "Solve real-world and mathematical problems involving perimeters of polygons, including finding the perimeter given the side lengths, finding an unknown side length, and exhibiting rectangles with the same perimeter and different areas or with the same area and different perimeters."

BACKGROUND

While the area of a polygon (a closed plane figure whose sides are line segments) is the number of square units needed to cover the flat surface, the perimeter of a polygon is the distance around the figure.

Two rectangles may have the same area but different perimeters. For example, a 4-by-5 rectangle and a 2-by-10 rectangle both have an area of 20 square units, but the perimeters are 18 units and 24 units respectively.

Two rectangles may have the same perimeters but different areas. For example, a 1-by-6 rectangle and a 3-by-4 rectangle both have a perimeter of 14 units, but their areas are 6 square units and 12 square units respectively.

 ## ACTIVITY 1: AREA AND FINDING PERIMETER

Working in pairs or groups of three, students will create rectangles with a given area and then find the perimeters.

MATERIALS

About 15 1-inch square color tiles; rulers; unlined paper; reproducible, "Areas and Perimeters of Rectangles," for each pair or group of students.

PROCEDURE

1. Explain that rectangles may have the same area but different perimeters. Sketch a 4-by-5 rectangle and a 2-by-10 rectangle on the board. Both have an area of 20 square units, but their perimeters are 18 units and 24 units.

2. Hand out copies of the reproducible. Explain that it contains instructions for creating rectangles that have a given area.

3. Explain that students are to first use their tiles to create the rectangles, working with one rectangle at a time. After they create a rectangle, they are to draw it on their unlined paper,

label each side, and find its perimeter. Be sure that students understand that a 1-by-2 rectangle, for example, is the same as a 2-by-1 rectangle. It is only positioned differently. In cases where there is more than one possible rectangle, students should provide drawings and perimeters for all of them. (If necessary, remind your students that a square is a special kind of rectangle.)

CLOSURE

Discuss students' sketches and perimeters. Ask: How did you find the perimeters of the rectangles when given the areas?

ANSWERS

The dimensions of the rectangles and their perimeters are listed in order. **(1)** 1 by 1, 4. **(2)** 1 by 2, 6. **(3)** 1 by 4, 10; 2 by 2, 8. **(4)** 1 by 5, 12. **(5)** 1 by 8, 18; 2 by 4, 12. **(6)** 1 by 9, 20; 3 by 3, 12. **(7)** 1 by 10, 22; 2 by 5, 14. **(8)** 1 by 12, 26; 2 by 6, 16; 3 by 4, 14

ACTIVITY 2: PERIMETER AND FINDING AREA

Working in pairs or groups of three, students will create rectangles with a given perimeter and then find the areas of the rectangles they created.

MATERIALS

About 20 1-inch square color tiles; rulers; unlined paper; reproducible, "Perimeters and Areas of Rectangles," for each pair or group of students.

PROCEDURE

1. Explain that rectangles may have the same perimeter but different areas. Sketch a 1-by-6 rectangle and a 3-by-4 rectangle on the board. Both have perimeters of 14 units but their areas are 6 square units and 12 square units.

2. Hand out copies of the reproducible. Explain that it contains instructions for creating rectangles that have a given perimeter.

3. Explain that students are to use their tiles to create rectangles that have the given perimeters, working with one rectangle at a time. After they create a rectangle, they are to draw it on their unlined paper, label its sides, and find its area. Be sure that students understand that a 1-by-2 rectangle, for example, is the same as a 2-by-1 rectangle. It is only positioned differently. In cases where there is more than one possible rectangle, students should provide drawings and areas for all of them. (If necessary, remind your students that a square is a special kind of rectangle.)

CLOSURE

Discuss students' sketches and areas. Ask: How did you find the dimensions of the rectangles when given the perimeters?

ANSWERS

The dimensions of the rectangles and the areas are listed in order. **(1)** 1 by 1, 1. **(2)** 1 by 2, 2. **(3)** 1 by 4, 4; 2 by 3, 6. **(4)** 1 by 5, 5; 2 by 4, 8; 3 by 3, 9. **(5)** 1 by 7, 7; 2 by 6, 12; 3 by 5, 15; 4 by 4, 16

  ## ACTIVITY 3: DESIGNING A VEGETABLE GARDEN

Working in small groups, students will design a vegetable garden with a given perimeter. They will then find the area of their garden.

MATERIALS

Graph paper; rulers for each group.

PROCEDURE

1. Explain that students are to design a vegetable garden. Because small animals, such as rabbits, like vegetables, students will need to place a wire fence around their garden. They have 50 feet of wire fence.

2. Explain that students should design a rectangular garden with a perimeter of 50 feet. They should consider and sketch several possible plans before choosing the one they want.

3. Explain that after students have agreed on a design for their garden, they should draw the plan on their graph paper. Suggest a scale of 1 unit on their graph paper equaling 1 foot of the garden. They are to label the lengths of the garden's sides (which must total 50), and then find the area of the garden.

CLOSURE

Have students share their garden designs with other groups. It is likely that the designs will vary. Discuss that although the perimeters of the gardens equal 50, the areas will vary, according to each garden's dimensions. Which garden had the largest area? Which had the smallest? Why?

Directions: Use square tiles to make the rectangles below. After you make each rectangle, draw it on a separate piece of paper. Then write the lengths of each side and find the perimeter.

1. Create a rectangle that has an area of 1 square unit.

2. Create a rectangle that has an area of 2 square units.

3. Create two rectangles that each has an area of 4 square units.

4. Create a rectangle that has an area of 5 square units.

5. Create two rectangles that each has an area of 8 square units.

6. Create two rectangles that each has an area of 9 square units.

7. Create two rectangles that each has an area of 10 square units.

8. Create three rectangles that each has an area of 12 square units.

Directions: Use square tiles to make the rectangles below. After you make each rectangle, draw it on a separate piece of paper. Then write the lengths of each side and find the area.

1. Create a rectangle that has a perimeter of 4 units.

2. Create a rectangle that has a perimeter of 6 units.

3. Create two rectangles that each has a perimeter of 10 units.

4. Create three rectangles that each has a perimeter of 12 units.

5. Create four rectangles that each has a perimeter of 16 units.

Geometry: 3.G.1

"Reason with shapes and their attributes."

1. "Understand that shapes in different categories (e.g., rhombuses, rectangles, and others) may share attributes (e.g., having four sides), and that the shared attributes can define a larger category (e.g., quadrilaterals). Recognize rhombuses, rectangles, and squares as examples of quadrilaterals, and draw examples of quadrilaterals that do no not belong to any of these subcategories."

BACKGROUND

Quadrilaterals (four-sided figures) have three subgroups: trapeziums, which have no parallel sides, parallelograms, which have two pairs of parallel and congruent sides, and trapezoids, which have only one pair of parallel sides.

Parallelograms have two subgroups: rhombuses, which have four congruent sides, and rectangles, which have two pairs of parallel sides, two pairs of congruent sides, and four right angles. A square, having four congruent sides and four right angles, is a rhombus *and* a rectangle.

Parallelogram serves both as an umbrella term over an entire category (as just described) and as a specific example within that category, namely, a quadrilateral with two pairs of parallel and congruent sides but no right angles. Likewise *rhombus* can refer either to a category of parallelogram that has four congruent sides that might or might not have right angles, or to a specific type of parallelogram with four congruent sides but no right angles.

ACTIVITY: CLASSIFYING QUADRILATERALS

Working in small groups, students will identify which quadrilateral does not belong in a set of three. They are to explain why they believe the figure selected does not belong and then draw a figure that does belong with the other two in the set.

MATERIALS

Scissors; glue sticks; rulers; unlined paper; reproducible, "Which One Does Not Belong?" for each group of students.

PROCEDURE

1. Explain that quadrilaterals can be classified in many ways: by the number of parallel sides, by the number of congruent sides, by the number of right angles, and by their perimeter and area.

2. If necessary, review the meanings of the following terms: parallel, congruent, right angle, perimeter, and area. Also, if necessary, provide examples of parallelograms, trapezoids, rhombuses, rectangles, and squares.

3. Hand out copies of the reproducible and explain that there are three figures in each row. Two belong in each set of three because they share some of the same features, but one does not. Students are to identify which figure does not belong with the other two and provide a reason why.

4. Use the first row as an example. Ask your students which figure does not belong with the other two. Students should say the square because it has four right angles.

5. Explain that once students have identified a figure that does not belong, they should write the number of the row and their reasons why the figure does not belong on a separate sheet of paper. They are to then draw a figure on unlined paper that belongs with the other two, cut the figure out, and glue it over the figure on the reproducible that does not belong. Using the first row as an example again, students should draw a rhombus that is not a square, cut it out, and glue it over the square so that every figure in the row has four congruent sides and no right angles. Instruct your students to follow this procedure for every row on the reproducible.

CLOSURE

Discuss the answers and share your students' correct responses.

Answers: The answer is provided for each problem, followed by placement and description of the sketch. **(1)** Figure two, the parallelogram, does not belong because it has two pairs of parallel sides while the other figures are trapezoids, which have one pair of parallel sides. A trapezoid should be placed over the second figure. **(2)** Figure two, the rhombus, does not belong because it has no right angles while the other figures have four right angles. A square should be placed over the second figure. **(3)** Figure three, the square, does not belong because it has four congruent sides while the other two figures have two pairs of congruent sides. A rectangle that is not a square should be placed over the third figure. **(4)** Figure one, the parallelogram, does not belong because it has two pairs of parallel sides while the other two figures are quadrilaterals that have no parallel sides. A quadrilateral with no parallel sides should be placed over the first figure.

WHICH ONE DOES NOT BELONG?

Example			
1.			
2.			
3.			
4.			

Geometry: 3.G.2

"Reason with shapes and their attributes."

> 2. "Partition shapes into parts with equal areas. Express the area of each part as a unit fraction of the whole."

BACKGROUND

Geometric figures can be partitioned into parts with equal areas. For example, a 2-by-2 square can be divided into four 1-by-1 squares. The area of each small square is $\frac{1}{4}$ of the area of the 2-by-2 square. The 2-by-2 square can also be partitioned into two 1-by-2 rectangles. The area of each rectangle is $\frac{1}{2}$ of the area of the square.

ACTIVITY: DECOMPOSING FIGURES

Working in pairs or groups of three, students will assemble parts of a geometric figure into the original figure. They will represent the area of each part as a unit fraction of the larger figure.

MATERIALS

Scissors; reproducibles, "Parts of Figures, I," "Parts of Figures, II," and "Geometric Figures," for each pair or group of students.

PROCEDURE

1. Distribute copies of the reproducibles. Explain that on "Parts of Figures, I" and "Parts of Figures, II" each group of figures in each box can be assembled to form one of the figures (a triangle, hexagon, square, or rectangle) contained on "Geometric Figures."

2. Explain that students should start with the figures in the first box. They should cut out the triangles and assemble them to form a figure shown on "Geometric Figures." After students have assembled the small figures, on a separate sheet of paper they should write the number of the box of the small figures, the fraction of the area each small figure makes up of the larger figure, and the name of the larger figure.

3. Instruct students to follow the same procedure for the figures in the other boxes.

CLOSURE

Discuss your student's results. Emphasize the unit fractions as parts of their wholes.

(1) The area of each part is $\frac{1}{4}$ of the area of the triangle. **(2)** The area of each part is $\frac{1}{4}$ of the area of the hexagon. **(3)** The area of each part is $\frac{1}{2}$ of the area of the hexagon. **(4)** The area of each part is $\frac{1}{2}$ of the area of the rectangle. **(5)** The area of each part is $\frac{1}{3}$ of the area of the rectangle. **(6)** The area of each part is $\frac{1}{8}$ of the area of the square. **(7)** The area of each part is $\frac{1}{4}$ of the area of the square. **(8)** The area of each part is $\frac{1}{2}$ of the area of the square.

1.

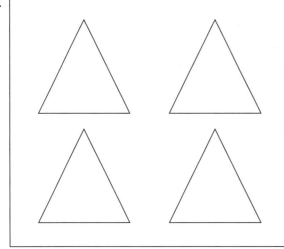

2.

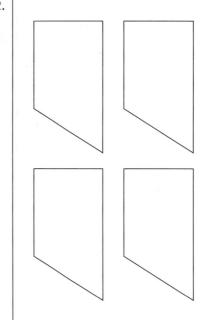

3.

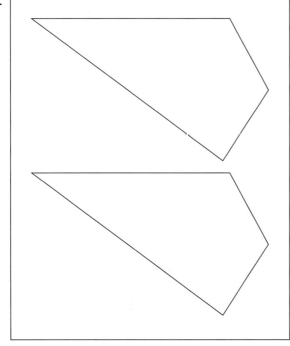

4.

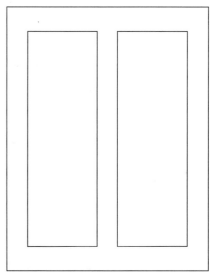

5.

6.

7.

8.

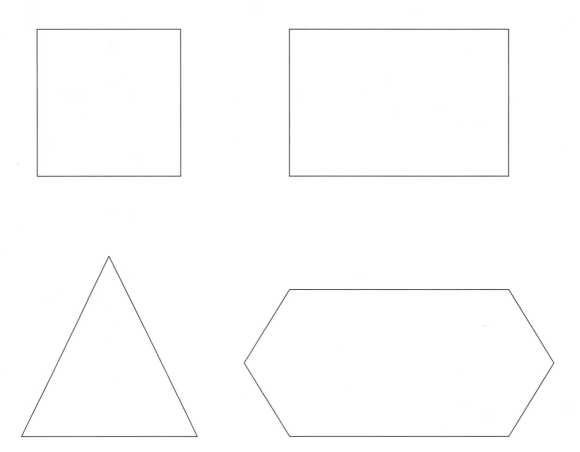

Standards and Activities for Grade 4

Operations and Algebraic Thinking: 4.OA.1

"Use the four operations with whole numbers to solve problems."

1. "Interpret a multiplication equation as a comparison, e.g., interpret $35 = 5 \times 7$ as a statement that 35 is 5 times as many as 7 and 7 times as many as 5. Represent verbal statements of multiplicative comparisons as multiplication equations."

BACKGROUND

Multiplication can be described as a comparison between the product and its factors. For example, $16 = 2 \times 8$ means 2 groups of 8. It also means that 16 is 2 times as many as 8 or 8 times as many as 2.

 ## ACTIVITY: MULTIPLICATION TIC-TAC-TOE

Working in pairs or groups of three, students will complete tic-tac-toe boards by writing equivalent multiplication statements. The first person to get three equivalent statements in a row or along a diagonal wins.

MATERIALS

Unlined paper for each student.

PROCEDURE

1. Explain that students will play multiplication tic-tac-toe, but note that this is a little different from the standard tic-tac-toe game.

2. Explain that prior to the game, each student will select a number from 2 to 50 as a product and write five equivalent multiplication statements about the product on a piece of paper. For example, suppose a student chooses the number 16. Some statements she could write are 8×2, 2×8, 8 groups of 2, 8 times as many as 2, or 4 times as many as 4.

3. Hand out the unlined paper. (If you are considering playing more than one round, you might have your students fold their papers in half from top to bottom. Using the front and back of the paper results in four regions, each of which can easily accommodate one tic-tac-toe board.) Instruct your students to draw a tic-tac-toe board as shown. Note that the boxes on the board should be large enough to accommodate multiplication statements.

4. Explain to your students that two students at a time are to play. The student who has the largest product goes first. She writes one of her multiplication statements in a box on the tic-tac-toe board. The other student then writes one of his multiplication statements. The first student to get three equivalent multiplication statements in a row or along a diagonal wins. Prior to declaring a winner, however, the other student must check that his opponent's multiplication statements are, in fact, correct. You may need to serve as referee in some instances.

5. Begin the games, following the procedure outlined above.

6. If time permits, play several rounds, with students selecting new products and writing new multiplication statements. Make sure that all students in groups of three have a chance to play.

CLOSURE

Discuss the number of equivalent multiplication statements students generated. Choose a product, and on the board write as many equivalent multiplication statements as the class can generate.

Operations and Algebraic Thinking: 4.OA.2

"Use the four operations with whole numbers to solve problems."

> 2. "Multiply or divide to solve word problems involving multiplicative comparison, e.g., by using drawings and equations with a symbol for the unknown number to represent the problem, distinguishing multiplicative comparison from additive comparison."

BACKGROUND

Word problems can be efficiently solved if students follow these steps:

1. Read the problem carefully.

2. Understand the problem, recognize what information is provided, and what they are asked to find. (For example, phrases such as "how many times more" indicate a multiplicative comparison, and questions such as "how many more" indicate an additive comparison. Recognizing the differences between such comparisons can help students choose the correct operation to solve the problem.)

3. Develop a plan to solve the problem. Equations and diagrams are useful tools. If students write an equation, encourage them to use a symbol to represent the unknown quantity.

4. Follow the plan to solve the problem.

5. Check for accuracy and that the answer is reasonable.

ACTIVITY: WHAT'S THE PROBLEM?

Students are to draw a picture and then write a word problem based on the picture that can be solved using multiplication or division. They will then exchange their picture and problem with another student and solve each other's problems.

MATERIALS

Drawing paper; crayons for each student.

PROCEDURE

1. For this activity, tell your students that they will use pictures as a starting point to write word problems that can be solved using multiplication or division.

2. As an example, suggest that students imagine a picture of 2 children and 4 cookies. Based on this picture, students might create the following problem: How many cookies could each child have if the cookies are shared equally?

3. Instruct your students to draw a picture in which groups having the same number per group must be combined (multiplied), or a total number of objects must be distributed equally (division).

4. Explain that after they have completed their picture, they are to write a word problem (based on their picture) that can be solved either by using multiplication or division. They should write their problem below their picture.

5. Instruct your students to exchange their picture and problem with those of another student. They are to write an equation with a symbol for an unknown number to represent the problem, and then solve the problem.

6. Remind students to read the problem carefully. Suggest that they use the picture to help them decide if the problem requires them to use multiplication or division to solve it.

CLOSURE

Have volunteers present their pictures and problems to the class. Have the class solve some of the problems as a group. Select a few pictures that students used to write multiplication problems. Ask your students to provide a word problem, based on the picture, that can be solved using an additive comparison instead of multiplication. You may also want to display the pictures and problems.

Operations and Algebraic Thinking: 4.0A.3

"Use the four operations with whole numbers to solve problems."

3. "Solve multistep word problems posed with whole numbers and having whole-number answers using the four operations, including problems in which remainders must be interpreted. Represent these problems using equations with a letter standing for the unknown quantity. Assess the reasonableness of answers using mental computation and estimation strategies including rounding."

BACKGROUND

Solving multistep word problems requires the same steps as solving simple word problems. Students must read the problem, understand the problem, plan how to solve it, carry out the plan, and check their answer.

Students must always be alert to the reasonableness of an answer. In division, sometimes remainders make no sense in the context of the problem. For example, consider a class of 26 students. If 6 students can sit at a table, how many tables must the classroom have? Simple division provides the quotient of 4 remainder 2. But if only 4 tables are provided, 2 students will not have seats. The reasonable answer is that 5 tables are needed.

 ## ACTIVITY: EQUATIONS AND PROBLEMS

Working in small groups, students will solve multistep word problems. They will write an equation, using a letter to stand for an unknown quantity, solve the equation, and determine if the answer is reasonable in the context of the problem.

MATERIALS

Scissors; one copy of the reproducible, "Problems and Reasonable Answers," for the teacher's use.

PREPARATION

Make a copy of the reproducible and cut out the word problems along the broken lines.

PROCEDURE

1. Divide your class into eight groups and explain that they will be working with eight word problems.

2. Hand out a different word problem slip to each group. Explain to your students that after reading the problem and determining what they are to find, they are to write an equation that can be used to solve their problem, using a letter to represent what they are trying to find. After solving the problem, they are to determine if their answer is reasonable. Caution them to interpret quotients that have remainders, if necessary. Allow time for students to work. Explain that students should do all their work on a separate sheet of paper, not the slip of paper containing their problem.

3. After all groups have solved their first problem, instruct your students to exchange their problems with another group. For example, the group that had problem 1 should pass their problem to the group that had problem 2, and the group that had problem 2 should pass their problem to the group that had problem 3, and so on. (*Note:* Having groups working on one problem at a time allows you to manage the activity more efficiently and helps to keep the groups focused.)

4. Make sure that all groups have a chance to solve all eight problems.

CLOSURE

Call on the final group that finished with problem 1 and ask them to present their work to the class. Have the other groups compare their work and make any corrections. Next call on the final group to finish problem 2, then problem 3, and so on until each problem has been presented. Note that different groups may have written different equations to solve some problems. Ask your students how they determined if their answers were reasonable.

ANSWER

Equations may vary; one equation is provided for each problem. (**1**) $n =$ Nadine's score; $n = (85 + 95) \div 2$; $n = 90$; (**2**) $b =$ the number of \$10 bills; $(85 - 5) \div 10 = b$; $b = 8$
(**3**) $t =$ the number of tables; $(1 + 28) \div 8 = t$; $t = 3$ r5; 4 tables are required
(**4**) $h =$ the number of additional hours Andrew parked; $(20 - 4) \div 2 = h$; $h = 8$; $8 + 1 = 9$
total hours (**5**) $c =$ the number of DVD cases; $(20 + 5) \div 12 = c$; $c = 2$ r1; 3 DVD cases are
needed (**6**) $b =$ the cost of the dog bowls; $33 - (15 + 12) = b$; $b = \$6$
(**7**) $t =$ the cost of Mason's ticket; $28 - (2 \times 10) = t$; $t = \$8$
(**8**) $d =$ the total distance Daniela walked; $1 + (2 \times 1) = d$; $d = 3$ miles

1. Arielle's math test score was 10 points higher than Scot's score. Scot's score was 85. Nadine's score was halfway between their scores. What was Nadine's score?

2. Riley has saved a $5 bill and some $10 bills. His total amount of money is $85. How many $10 bills does he have?

3. Marcus is planning a party for his little sister. He can get tables that each seat 8 people. His sister has 28 friends coming to the party. How many tables must Marcus have for his sister and her friends?

4. Andrew parked his car in a parking garage. It cost $4 for the first hour and $2 for each additional hour. Andrew paid $20 for parking. How many hours was his car parked?

5. Audrey wants to store her DVDs in cases. She has 20 DVDs and plans to buy 5 more. Each case holds 12 DVDs. How many cases will she need?

6. Ethan adopted a dog. He spent $15 on dog food and $12 for toys. He also bought dog bowls for food and water. In all, he spent $33. How much did the dog bowls cost?

7. Mason spent $28 for two adult tickets and one student ticket for the school play. The adult tickets cost $10 each. How much did Mason's ticket cost?

8. Daniela is starting a walking program. She walked a mile the first day. She walked twice as far the second day. What is the total distance she walked?

Operations and Algebraic Thinking: 4.OA.4

"Gain familiarity with factors and multiples."

> 4. "Find all factor pairs for a whole number in the range 1–100. Recognize that a whole number is a multiple of each of its factors. Determine whether a given whole number in the range 1–100 is a multiple of a given one-digit number. Determine whether a given whole number in the range 1–100 is prime or composite."

BACKGROUND

Every number except 1 has two or more factors. A number that has only two factors, 1 and the number, is a prime number. A number that has more than two factors is a composite number.

Composite numbers can be expressed as the product of two or more pairs of factors. For example, 30 is a composite number. Its pairs of factors are 1×30, 2×15, 3×10, and 5×6. These pairs of factors can be rewritten as 30×1, 15×2, 10×3, and 6×5. The pairs are the same; only the order of the numbers is reversed.

The prime numbers that are less than 100 are: 2, 3, 5, 7, 11, 13, 17, 19, 23, 29, 31, 37, 41, 43, 47, 53, 59, 61, 67, 71, 73, 79, 83, 89, and 97. (1 is neither prime nor composite.) All other numbers that are less than 100 are composite numbers.

 ## ACTIVITY: THE PRIME CHALLENGE

Working in small groups, students will play the game "The Prime Challenge," in which they will identify prime and composite numbers.

MATERIALS

Pens; one 4-inch-by-6-inch index card for each group of students; a dark marker for the teacher.

PREPARATION

Make a number card to easily identify groups. Fold the index cards in half, resembling a tent. Use a marker to label each card with Group 1, Group 2, and so on until each group has a number. On a sheet of paper, make a score sheet with group numbers labeled in each column, as shown below. (*Note:* You may have more than six groups.)

Group 1	Group 2	Group 3	Group 4	Group 5	Group 6

PROCEDURE

1. Distribute the group number cards, one to each group. Students should place the card on their desk so that you can easily see the group number to facilitate scoring.

2. Ask each group of students to use a pen to write any 10 numbers between 1 and 100 on a sheet of paper. (*Note:* Using a pen prevents students from changing their numbers.)

3. Instruct each group to circle the prime numbers from the numbers they wrote. When called upon, they will read the prime numbers they circled.

4. Explain the rules. You will call on one group at a time. A group member will read the first prime number that the group circled. The other groups must agree or disagree if the number is a prime number. If a group disagrees, it must show a correct pair of factors. Following is an example of the scoring process, using Group 1:

   - If Group 1 is correct, and the other groups agree, Group 1 gets 10 points.

   - If Group 1 is correct, but a group feels that Group 1 is incorrect, the other group must offer a pair of factors to show why the number is not prime. If the first disagreeing group is incorrect, they lose 10 points. Likewise, if another group disagrees and is incorrect, they also lose 10 points. Group 1 gets 10 points.

   - If Group 1 is incorrect, the first group to disagree and state a correct pair of factors gains 10 points. Group 1 then loses 10 points.

   - If Group 1 is incorrect and no other groups disagree, or if disagreeing groups cannot provide a correct pair of factors, you provide the factors and all groups lose 10 points.

5. Offer this example: Suppose Group 1 said 29, and no other group disagreed. Group 1 gets 10 points. If Group 1 said 29 and another group disagrees, Group 1 gets 10 points for being correct. The group that disagreed loses 10 points. If Group 1 said 12 is prime, which is incorrect, the first team to disagree and show a correct pair of factors gains 10 points. Group 1 also loses 10 points. If Group 1 said 12 is prime and no other group disagrees, all teams lose 10 points.

6. Begin the competition with Group 1. Ask them to read the first prime number they circled. Ask if the class agrees. If there is disagreement, call on the first group that disagrees. If the disagreeing group presents incorrect factors, call on the next group that disagrees to present correct factors. Once correct factors are presented, award points and mark them on your score sheet.

7. Now go to Group 2 and ask them to state the first prime number they circled. Follow the same procedure, and then move on to the other groups.

8. After all the groups have stated their first prime number and all points have been awarded, return to Group 1 and ask them to state their second prime number. In instances where the prime number a group has circled has already been used, simply have them move on to their next circled prime. If a group uses all of their prime numbers and the game is not finished, they can still participate by agreeing or disagreeing with the other groups.

9. Continue the procedure until all prime numbers have been read.

CLOSURE

Tally the scores and declare a winner. Do a special bonus round. Present at least three composite numbers, one at time, from 1 through 100. Ask the groups to list all of the one-digit numbers (other than 1) that the composite number is a multiple of. For example, 35 is a multiple of 5 and 7; 64 is a multiple of 2, 4, and 8. (*Note:* 64 is also a multiple of 16 and 32, but 16 and 32 are not one-digit numbers and should not be listed.) Present a number and have groups write their answer on a sheet of paper, and then turn their paper face down. Ask each group one at a time to reveal the answers they wrote on their paper. Groups receive one point for naming each one-digit number of which a composite number is a multiple. For instance, for 35, if students name 5 and 7, they receive two points. For 64, if they only name 2 and 8, they receive two points. For each incorrect number, they lose a point.

Operations and Algebraic Thinking: 4.OA.5

"Generate and analyze patterns."

> 5. "Generate a number or shape pattern that follows a given rule. Identify apparent features of the pattern that were not explicit in the rule itself."

BACKGROUND

A hundreds chart is a useful tool that can be used to generate a variety of numbers. These numbers depend upon the starting number and the number that is added to it.

The patterns that can be generated can surprise students. For example, sometimes a pattern will generate only even numbers. Starting with 2 and adding 2 results in a pattern of 2, 4, 6, 8, ... Sometimes a pattern will generate only odd numbers. Starting with 1 and adding 6 results in 1, 7, 13, 19, ... And sometimes a pattern will generate even and odd numbers. Starting with 2 and adding 3 results in a pattern of 2, 5, 8, 11, ...

 ACTIVITY: NUMBER GENERATOR

Working individually or in pairs, students will virtually create and identify numbers on a hundreds chart.

MATERIALS

Computers with Internet access for students; computer with Internet access and digital projector for the teacher.

PROCEDURE

1. Explain that students will generate number patterns on a hundreds chart. A hundreds chart is a list of numbers ranging from 1 to 100 arranged on a 10-by-10 grid.

2. Instruct students to go to http://nlvm.usu.edu. They should click in the grades "3–5" column on the "Number and Operations" row and then scroll down and click on "Hundreds Chart."

3. Once students have the hundreds chart on their screens, explain that at the top of the chart is "Count By" and "Starting At." Students can decide what number to start at by using the up or down arrow. To decide what number to count by, they can also use the up or down arrow. After they have decided on their numbers, they should click on "Practice" at the bottom of the grid. (*Note:* This might already be selected.)

4. Explain that students should now click on the number they chose to start with, and then click on the next number that they chose to count by. For example, if a student decided to start with 4 and count by 3, she would click on 4, 7, 10, 13, 16, … Correct numbers in a pattern will be colored blue; incorrect numbers will be colored red.

5. Ask your students to explain the pattern. (*Note:* Clicking on "Show" will show the pattern up to 100 and clicking on "Animate" will show the progression of the pattern.)

6. Instruct your students to click on "Clear" to clear the grid and start the procedure again.

7. Allow time for your students to explore various patterns. Students should record some of the patterns they explore so that they may share them during the closure.

CLOSURE

Ask your students to explain the patterns they found. Ask volunteers to suggest other numbers to start with and count by. Input this data on the hundreds chart and click on "Animate" to generate the pattern. Discuss the patterns.

Number and Operations in Base Ten: 4.NBT.1

"Generalize place value understanding for multi-digit whole numbers."

1. "Recognize that in a multi-digit whole number, a digit in one place represents ten times what it represents in the place to its right."

BACKGROUND

The value of a digit depends on its place in a number. For example, the value of 9 in 94 is 90; the value of 9 in 937 is 900. The value of a digit in one place is ten times the value of the digit in the place to its right.

 ### ACTIVITY: MAKING MODELS OF PLACE VALUE

Students will work in groups to create a place-value model, showing values in the ones, tens, and hundreds places. The class will then create a place-value model showing values in the one, tens, hundreds, and thousands places.

MATERIALS

Scissors; glue sticks; four copies of reproducible, "Picture Pencils," for each group of students. Optional: Card stock; masking tape or mounting tape for the teacher.

PREPARATION

To create the class place-value model, you will need an area of about 15 square feet, or about three feet by five feet. You may use the board, your classroom floor, a wall in a hallway, or a similar flat surface.

PROCEDURE

1. Divide your class into ten groups and explain that each group will make a place-value model, using a certain number of "picture" pencils to show the value of each place. Students will then work as a class to complete a larger place-value model.

2. Distribute four copies of the reproducible to each group.

3. Instruct students to cut out 1 pencil. This represents 1. They should set it aside for now.

4. Instruct students to form a column of 10 pencils. Suggest that they cut out two pencils from the reproducible they used for cutting out the pencil for the ones place. Instruct students to glue the two pencils at the bottom of a column on another of the reproducibles. This column now represents tens. They should cut out this column and set it aside.

5. Instruct students to make 10 columns of 10, which represent 100. They should glue the columns together (along their edges). Suggest that they cut out two rows of pencils from two of the copies and glue them at the bottom of the columns of eight pencils on the other two copies, to create 10 rows.

6. Instruct students to place their 1 pencil, column of 10 pencils, and columns of 100 pencils beside each other on a desk. Explain that they have a created a place value model for ones, tens, and hundreds. Emphasize that the value of each place represents 10 times the value of the place to its right.

7. Explain that, as a class, you will now construct a place value model for ones, tens, hundreds, and thousands.

8. Start with the ones. Ask a student to attach 1 pencil (with masking tape, mounting tape, or other material) to the surface on which you will display the model. This represents the ones place.

9. Next ask a student to attach a column of 10 on the surface for the model. This column represents the tens place.

10. Now ask for volunteers to attach 10 columns of 10 on the surface. These columns represent the hundreds place.

11. Ask how many groups of 100 are needed to make 1,000. Students should answer 10. Ask for volunteers to attach 10 groups of 100 to the surface. These groups represent the thousands place.

12. Use card stock to label each place value, and attach the labels above the proper columns to complete a place value chart of ones, tens, hundreds, and thousands. Seeing the visual representation will help students to understand the powers of 10.

CLOSURE

Ask students if they were surprised by the quantities in each group. Why or why not? Ask: How do the quantities change as you move in place value from right to left? Left to right? Emphasize that a digit in one place is 10 times what it represents in the place to its right.

PICTURE PENCILS

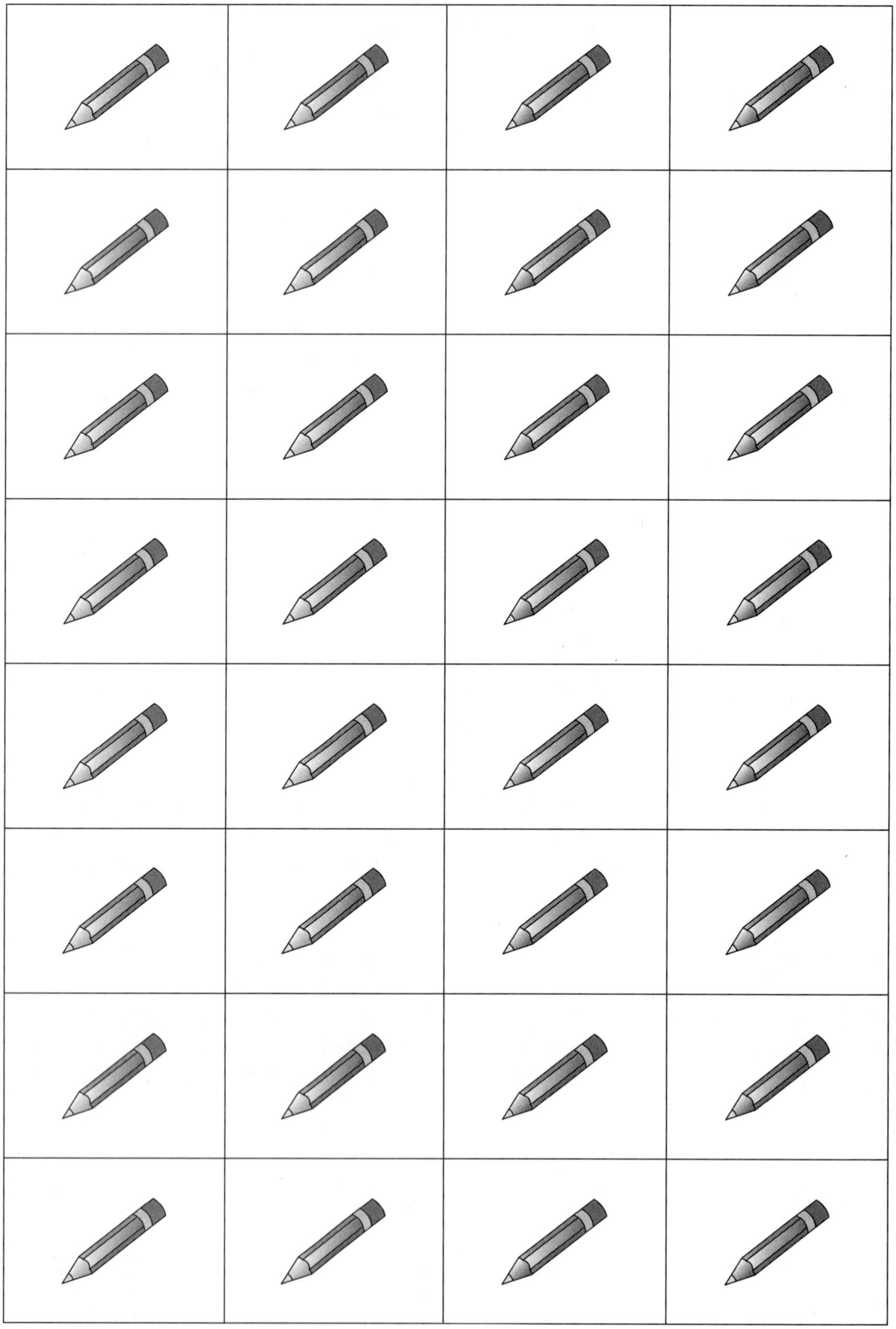

Number and Operations in Base Ten: 4.NBT.2

"Generalize place value understanding for multi-digit whole numbers."

> 2. "Read and write multi-digit whole numbers using base-ten numerals, number names, and expanded form. Compare two multi-digit numbers based on meanings of the digits in each place, using >, =, and < symbols to record the results of comparisons."

BACKGROUND

Numbers can be represented in three ways: word form, numerical form, or in expanded form. For example:

- Word form: Fifty-two thousand, six hundred forty-nine
- Numerical form: 52,649
- Expanded form: 50,000 + 2,000 + 600 + 40 + 9

ACTIVITY: EXPRESSING NUMBERS

Working in pairs or groups of three, students will represent a number in three different forms. They will then select any two pairs of numbers and compare them using the inequality symbols, > or < .

MATERIALS

Scissors; glue sticks; one sheet of large construction paper; reproducible, "Number Form Cards," for each pair or group of students.

PROCEDURE

1. Distribute copies of the reproducible and explain that it contains eight rows. The first six rows contain six cards each, and the last two rows contain three cards each. The cards in the first row contain numbers in standard form. The cards in the second through sixth rows contain parts of the numbers, written in expanded form. When combined correctly, they will match the numbers in the first row. The cards in the last two rows contain the word forms of numbers in the first row.

2. Explain that students should cut out the cards.

3. Next explain that they are to arrange the cards on their construction paper so that each number in the first row is represented by its expanded form and word form.

4. After arranging their cards, students should glue them on their construction paper.

5. Explain that after gluing their cards, students are to compare two pairs of the numbers they worked with. One pair of numbers is to be compared using the > symbol. The other pair of numbers is to be compared using the < symbol. Students should write their comparisons at the bottom of their construction paper.

CLOSURE

Discuss students' results.

ANSWERS

- $2,345 = 2,000 + 300 + 40 + 5 =$ two thousand, three hundred forty-five

- $106,786 = 100,000 + 6,000 + 700 + 80 + 6 =$ one hundred six thousand, seven hundred eighty-six

- $859 = 800 + 50 + 9 =$ eight hundred fifty-nine

- $925,213 = 900,000 + 20,000 + 5,000 + 200 + 10 + 3 =$ nine hundred twenty-five thousand, two hundred thirteen

- $654,124 = 600,000 + 50,000 + 4,000 + 100 + 20 + 4 =$ six hundred fifty-four thousand, one hundred twenty-four

- $341,631 = 300,000 + 40,000 + 1,000 + 600 + 30 + 1 =$ three hundred forty-one thousand, six hundred thirty-one

- Comparisons may vary. Two correct answers are $925,213 > 654,124$ and $859 < 2,345$.

NUMBER FORM CARDS

2,345	106,786	859	925,213	654,124	341,631
300 +	900,000 +	300,000 +	30 +	700 +	20 +
1	600,000 +	200 +	100,000 +	6	20,000 +
10 +	5	2,000 +	9	800 +	3
4,000 +	80 +	40 +	50,000 +	100 +	600 +
1,000 +	4	5,000 +	40,000 +	50 +	6,000+
Nine hundred twenty-five thousand, two hundred thirteen		Two thousand, three hundred forty-five		Eight hundred fifty-nine	
Six hundred fifty-four thousand, one hundred twenty-four		Three hundred forty-one thousand, six hundred thirty-one		One hundred six thousand, seven hundred eighty-six	

Number and Operations in Base Ten: 4.NBT.3

"Generalize place value understanding for multi-digit whole numbers."

3. "Use place value understanding to round multi-digit whole numbers to any place."

BACKGROUND

An understanding of place value is essential to rounding numbers. To round a number, students must first find the digit to the right of the place they are rounding to. They must then follow the rules for rounding:

- If the digit to the right of the digit to be rounded is less than 5, the digit in the place to be rounded stays the same. Change any digits to the right of that digit to zero.

- If the digit to the right of the digit to be rounded is 5 or more, add 1 to the digit in the place to be rounded. Change any digits to the right of that digit to zero.

- If 9 is in the place to be rounded, and the number to its right is less than 5, 9 stays the same. Change any digits to its right to zero. If the number to the right of 9 is 5 or more, add 1 to the 9. Because $1 + 9 = 10$, change 9 to zero and add 1 to the digit to the left. Change any digits to the right of the rounded number to zero.

ACTIVITY: ROUNDING NUMBERS

This is a two-day activity. Working in groups, students will be given two numbers. They will create a poster on the first day and, using their poster as a visual aid on the second day, will explain to the class how to round the two numbers they were given.

MATERIALS

Large poster paper; rulers; markers; crayons for each group.

PROCEDURE

Day One

1. Review the steps for rounding with your students. Provide some examples, such as the following:

   - Round 375 to the nearest ten: 380.

   - Round 6,436 to the nearest hundred: 6,400.

   - Round 58,721 to the nearest thousand: 59,000.

2. Explain that each group will be given two numbers, one that must be rounded up and one that must be rounded down. Students will detail the procedure for rounding each on poster paper and then present their work to the class.

3. Suggest that students brainstorm ideas on how to design their posters before beginning work. To clarify their ideas, they should do a "rough" design on a separate sheet of paper first.

4. Provide each group with two numbers. You may select numbers of your own or you can use these:

1. Round 8,576 to the nearest hundred.	Round 26,753 to the nearest ten.
2. Round 4,684 to the nearest ten.	Round 73,165 to the nearest hundred.
3. Round 9,029 to the nearest ten.	Round 91,484 to the nearest thousand.
4. Round 14,783 to the nearest hundred.	Round 9,238 to the nearest thousand.
5. Round 4,958 to the nearest ten.	Round 35,029 to the nearest thousand.
6. Round 75,483 to the nearest thousand.	Round 6,294 to the nearest hundred.
7. Round 95,951 to the nearest hundred.	Round 8,502 to the nearest ten.
8. Round 42,075 to the nearest ten.	Round 8,146 to the nearest thousand.
9. Round 54,899 to the nearest ten.	Round 4,816 to the nearest hundred.
10. Round 19,843 to the nearest hundred.	Round 6,503 to the nearest thousand.

5. Caution students to round their numbers correctly. They should arrive at a consensus for their answers before they begin their posters.

6. Encourage them to be creative but accurate. Their posters should clearly detail the steps for rounding with their example problems.

7. Collect the posters at the end of class.

Day Two

1. Hand the posters back to each group.

2. Provide a few minutes for students to organize their presentations.

Have each group share their posters with the class and explain how they rounded their numbers. The posters should serve as visual aids.

ANSWERS

(1) 8,600; 26,750 **(2)** 4,680; 73,200 **(3)** 9,030; 91,000 **(4)** 14,800; 9,000 **(5)** 4,960; 35,000 **(6)** 75,000; 6,300 **(7)** 96,000; 8,500 **(8)** 42,080; 8,000 **(9)** 54,900; 4,800 **(10)** 19,800; 7,000

Number and Operations in Base Ten: 4.NBT.4

"Use place value understanding and properties of operations to perform multi-digit arithmetic."

> 4. "Fluently add and subtract multi-digit whole numbers using the standard algorithm."

BACKGROUND

The most efficient way to add and subtract multi-digit whole numbers is to line up the digits according to place value. Students should start with the ones, and then work with the tens, hundreds, thousands, and so on. They should regroup, if necessary. To make sure that an answer makes sense, students should estimate their answer before adding or subtracting, and then compare their answer with their estimate.

 ### ACTIVITY: A NUMBERS CHAIN

Working in pairs or groups of three, students will complete addition and subtraction problems whose answers are related in a chain.

MATERIALS

Scissors; glue sticks; reproducible, "Sums and Differences," for each pair or group of students.

PROCEDURE

1. Distribute copies of the reproducible. Explain that Column I and Column II show numbers; addition, subtraction, and equal symbols; and empty boxes. On the right side of the reproducible is a column of number cards.

2. Explain that students are to cut out the number cards. They are to place the number cards in the empty boxes of the first column so that the column continues as a chain and ends equaling 36,725. They are to do the same with the second column, although this time the chain ends with 448,296.

3. Instruct your students to place each of the number cards in its correct box in either Column I or Column II. They are then to glue the cards in their appropriate boxes.

Discuss students' answers and the strategies they used to complete the chains.

ANSWERS

Column I: 341; 7,438; 17,917; 1,637; 6,516; 30,209
Column II: 116,269; 92,691; 23,125; 3,753; 484,817; 36,521

SUMS AND DIFFERENCES

Column I

238

+ [ ]

= 579

+ 6,859

= [ ]

+ 10,479

= [ ]

− [ ]

= 16,280

− 9,764

= [ ]

+ [ ]

= 36,725

Column II

169,205

− 52,936

= [ ]

− 23,578

= [ ]

+ [ ]

= 115,816

+ [ ]

= 119,569

+ 365,248

= [ ]

− [ ]

= 448,296

Number Cards	
341	23,125
1,637	30,209
3,753	36,521
6,516	92,691
7,438	116,269
17,917	484,817

Number and Operations in Base Ten: 4.NBT.5

"Use place value understanding and properties of operations to perform multi-digit arithmetic."

> 5. "Multiply a whole number of up to four digits by a one-digit whole number, and multiply two two-digit numbers, using strategies based on place value and the properties of operations. Illustrate and explain the calculation by using equations, rectangular arrays, and/or area models."

BACKGROUND

Multiplication is a process in which numbers are multiplied according to place value. Following is an example:

$$\begin{array}{r} 56 \\ \times\ 24 \\ \hline 224 \\ +\ 1{,}120 \\ \hline 1{,}344 \end{array}$$

1. Multiply by the 4 ones. $4 \times 56 = 224$. This is the same as 4 groups of 56.
2. Multiply by the 2 tens. $20 \times 56 = 1{,}120$. This is the same as 20 groups of 56.
3. Add the partial products. $224 + 1{,}120 = 1{,}344$.

ACTIVITY 1: FINDING ERRORS IN MULTIPLICATION

Students will find and correct errors in multiplication problems. Then they will select one incorrect problem, write the correct product, and explain the procedure for finding the product using place value.

MATERIALS

One copy of reproducible, "Finding Errors," for each student.

PROCEDURE

1. Review the process of multiplication with your students.
2. Hand out copies of the reproducible. Explain that it contains 12 problems. Some problems are correct, but others have errors. Students are to find the errors in the incorrect problems and correct them.
3. Explain that after correcting the problems, students are to choose one of the problems they corrected and write an explanation of how to find the correct product using place value.

ANSWERS

Numbers 1, 4, 6, and 11 are correct. The answers to the incorrect problems follow:
(2) 16,394 **(3)** 7,792 **(5)** 432 **(7)** 1,400 **(8)** 2,304 **(9)** 2,035 **(10)** 2,976 **(12)** 1,073. Explanations for finding the correct product using place value will vary.

 ACTIVITY 2: STEPPING FORWARD WITH MULTIPLICATION

Working in groups, students will select two multiplication problems, find their products, and illustrate the process of multiplication.

MATERIALS

Rulers; markers; crayons; large drawing paper for each group.

PROCEDURE

1. Explain to your students that they are to provide two multiplication problems of their own. One is to be a four-digit number multiplied by a one-digit number, and the other is to be a two-digit number multiplied by a two-digit number. Two examples are $3,465 \times 7$ and 62×35.

2. Explain that students are to find the product of each problem. Remind them to double-check their work to make certain that their answers are correct before they begin work illustrating the process of multiplication.

3. Explain that they are to show the steps they used to find the products on their drawing paper. They should provide detailed steps, with examples that highlight place value and use equations, similar to the example provided in the Background.

4. Suggest to your students that they discuss possible designs and methods before beginning. They might do a "rough" draft of their ideas on a sheet of paper.

5. Encourage your students to be creative but accurate.

CLOSURE

Discuss students' work and allow groups to show their work to other groups. Display students' work.

Name _____ Date _____

FINDING ERRORS

Directions: Some of the problems below have errors. Find the mistakes and correct them. Then choose one of the problems you corrected. Write an explanation of how to find the product using place value.

1. $\begin{array}{r} 124 \\ \times\ 5 \\ \hline 620 \end{array}$	2. $\begin{array}{r} 2{,}342 \\ \times\ 7 \\ \hline 16{,}284 \end{array}$	3. $\begin{array}{r} 974 \\ \times\ 8 \\ \hline 7{,}782 \end{array}$	4. $\begin{array}{r} 1{,}076 \\ \times\ 9 \\ \hline 9{,}684 \end{array}$
5. $\begin{array}{r} 27 \\ \times\ 16 \\ \hline 162 \\ +270 \\ \hline 422 \end{array}$	6. $\begin{array}{r} 4{,}365 \\ \times\ 6 \\ \hline 26{,}190 \end{array}$	7. $\begin{array}{r} 35 \\ \times\ 40 \\ \hline 35 \\ +1420 \\ \hline 1455 \end{array}$	8. $\begin{array}{r} 196 \\ \times\ 24 \\ \hline 364 \\ +1{,}920 \\ \hline 2{,}284 \end{array}$
9. $\begin{array}{r} 37 \\ \times\ 55 \\ \hline 185 \\ +1850 \\ \hline 2{,}045 \end{array}$	10. $\begin{array}{r} 96 \\ \times\ 31 \\ \hline 91 \\ 185 \\ +2880 \\ \hline 2{,}971 \end{array}$	11. $\begin{array}{r} 27 \\ \times\ 42 \\ \hline 54 \\ 185 \\ +1080 \\ \hline 1{,}134 \end{array}$	12. $\begin{array}{r} 137 \\ \times\ 29 \\ \hline 243 \\ +740 \\ \hline 983 \end{array}$

Number and Operations in Base Ten: 4.NBT.6

"Use place value understanding and properties of operations to perform multi-digit arithmetic."

> 6. "Find whole-number quotients and remainders with up to four-digit dividends and one-digit divisors, using strategies based on place value, the properties of operations, and/or the relationship between multiplication and division. Illustrate and explain the calculation by using equations, rectangular arrays, and/or area models."

BACKGROUND

In division, the number you are dividing by is the *divisor*, the number you are dividing is the *dividend*, and the answer is the *quotient*. Students should be familiar with these terms. Because multiplication and division are inverse operations, students can easily check the quotient of a division problem by multiplying the quotient by the divisor and adding any remainder.

 ACTIVITY 1: DEMONSTRATING DIVISION

Working in pairs or groups of three, students will demonstrate their understanding of division by creating a word problem that can be solved by dividing a multi-digit number by a one-digit number. They will exchange problems with another group, and then write an equation and create a rectangular array to represent the problem. Finally, they will solve the problem by using the division algorithm.

MATERIALS

Graph paper for students; overhead projector; markers; transparency with a grid that contains at least 120 squares for the teacher.

PROCEDURE

1. Explain that division is the process of breaking up a number of items to find how many equal groups can be made, or how many items are in each group. Be sure that students understand the terms divisor, dividend, and quotient.

2. Provide this example: Deanna is counting the days until her family's vacation. Her family will leave in 120 days. How many weeks is this? Ask students what this question asks them to find. (They are finding the number of groups in terms of "weeks." There are seven days in each week.)

3. Represent the problem with an equation: $120 \div 7 = n$.

4. Model this on the transparency and overhead projector. Mark off 120 squares and divide them into groups with 7 in each group. (There are 17 groups of 7, with 1 square left over.)

5. Divide 120 by 7, using the division algorithm. The quotient is 17 remainder 1, which means her family will leave in 17 weeks and 1 day.

6. Instruct your students to create a word problem of their own that can be solved by dividing a multi-digit number by a one-digit number. Suggest that students limit the dividends in their problems to less than 200; otherwise they might have an unwieldy number of groups on their arrays. Check that students' problems are reasonable.

7. Instruct your students to exchange their problem for the problem of another group. They are to write an equation that represents the problem, draw an array on graph paper, and then solve the problem using long division, as in the example you provided.

CLOSURE

Have students return the problems, and confirm that the quotients, equations, and arrays are correct.

ACTIVITY 2: DIVISION PUZZLES

Working in pairs or groups of three, students will find missing quotients or missing dividends.

MATERIALS

Reproducible, "Dividends and Quotients," for each pair or group of students.

PROCEDURE

1. Distribute copies of the reproducible and explain that it contains 12 problems, each with a missing number. Along the right-hand side are 14 answers that can be dividends, quotients, and remainders.

2. Explain that students are to complete the problems by finding the missing numbers. They are to choose their answers from the numbers on the right-hand side of the page. Note that for two problems, students must find both quotients and remainders.

3. Explain that after students have correctly matched quotients and dividends with problems, they should write the answer in the proper place in each problem.

Review the correct answers. Discuss the strategies students used to match answers with problems.

ANSWERS

(1) 39 r4 **(2)** 52 r3 **(3)** 826 **(4)** 6,359 **(5)** 2,478 **(6)** 2,072 **(7)** 3,069 **(8)** 3,535 **(9)** 524 **(10)** 1,567 **(11)** 846 **(12)** 7,643

Problems | Answers

1. $8\overline{)316}$	2. $263 \div 5 = n$	39
		52
3. $4\overline{)3{,}304}$	4. $9\overline{)}\,^{706\ r5}$	524
		826
		846
5. $7\overline{)}\,^{354}$	6. $n \div 8 = 259$	1,567
		2,072
7. $6{,}138 \div 2 = n$	8. $6\overline{)}\,^{589\ r1}$	2,478
		3,069
9. $4\overline{)}\,^{131}$	10. $n \div 3 = 522\ r1$	3,535
		6,359
		7,643
11. $6\overline{)5{,}076}$	12. $n \div 7 = 1{,}091\ r6$	r3
		r4

Number and Operations—Fractions: 4.NF.1

"Extend understanding of fraction equivalence and ordering."

1. "Explain why a fraction $\frac{a}{b}$ is equivalent to a fraction $\frac{(n \times a)}{(n \times b)}$ by using visual fraction models, with attention to how the number and size of the parts differ even though the two fractions themselves are the same size. Use this principle to recognize and generate equivalent fractions."

BACKGROUND

Equivalent fractions are fractions that name the same number or amount. Every fraction is equivalent to fractions that can be generated by multiplying or dividing the numerator and denominator by the same non-zero number. Following are two examples:

- $\frac{6}{10} = \frac{6 \times 2}{10 \times 2} = \frac{12}{20}$
- $\frac{6}{10} = \frac{6 \div 2}{10 \div 2} = \frac{3}{5}$

 ## ACTIVITY: FINDING EQUIVALENT FRACTIONS

Working in pairs or groups of three on a Web site, students will generate equivalent fractions.

MATERIALS

Computers with Internet access for students; computer with Internet access and digital projector for the teacher.

PROCEDURE

1. Instruct students to go to http://nlvm.usu.edu/. They should click in the grades "3–5" column on the "Number and Operations" row and then scroll down and click on "Fractions-Equivalent."

2. Explain that students will see a circle, square, or rectangle divided into equal parts. Some of the parts will be shaded. They will also see a fraction relating the number of shaded parts to the total number of parts.

3. Demonstrate how to find a new name for the fraction by using the arrow button to select the number of parts. The up arrow divides the figure into a larger number of equal parts. The down arrow divides the figure into a smaller number of equal parts.

- Show your students that when the figure is divided into the correct number of parts, the shading will cover equal-sized parts entirely with no overlaps. The number of shaded parts represents the numerator. The number of equal parts represents the denominator. Note that students may recognize equivalent fractions without having to move the up and down arrows. In this case, they may simply enter the numerator and denominator in the spaces after the equal sign and then check their answers.

- Students are to complete the equivalence, and the computer will state if the equivalence is correct. If students are incorrect, the computer will provide hints for completing the equivalence correctly.

4. Instruct students to click on "New Fraction."

5. Allow time for your students to explore at least five different fractions, writing two equivalent fractions for each. Students should record their answers so that they may refer to them during Closure.

CLOSURE

Discuss students' results. Ask your students to write an explanation of how they can tell that two fractions are equivalent.

Number and Operations—Fractions: 4.NF.2

"Extend understanding of fraction equivalence and ordering."

2. "Compare two fractions with different numerators and different denominators, e.g., by creating common denominators or numerators, or by comparing to a benchmark fraction such as $\frac{1}{2}$. Recognize that comparisons are valid only when the two fractions refer to the same whole. Record the results of comparisons with symbols >, =, or <, and justify the conclusions, e.g., by using a visual fraction model."

BACKGROUND

Students may compare fractions in three ways:

- Find the common denominator and write equivalent fractions. Then they can compare the numerators. For example, if a student is asked to compare $\frac{3}{4}$ and $\frac{5}{8}$, she may say that $\frac{3}{4} = \frac{6}{8}$ and realize that because $\frac{6}{8} > \frac{5}{8}$, $\frac{3}{4} > \frac{5}{8}$.

- Create a model, comparing $\frac{3}{5}$ to $\frac{7}{10}$, as shown below.

1									
$\frac{1}{10}$	$\frac{1}{10}$	$\frac{1}{10}$	$\frac{1}{10}$	$\frac{1}{10}$	$\frac{1}{10}$	$\frac{1}{10}$	$\frac{1}{10}$	$\frac{1}{10}$	$\frac{1}{10}$
$\frac{1}{5}$		$\frac{1}{5}$		$\frac{1}{5}$		$\frac{1}{5}$		$\frac{1}{5}$	

$$\frac{3}{5} < \frac{7}{10}$$

- Compare a fraction to another fraction. For example, $\frac{1}{3}$ can be compared to $\frac{3}{5}$ by understanding that $\frac{1}{3} < \frac{1}{2}$ and $\frac{3}{5} > \frac{1}{2}$; therefore $\frac{1}{3} < \frac{3}{5}$.

ACTIVITY: COMPARING FRACTIONS

Working in pairs or groups of three, students will select values from fraction cards, and, using comparison symbols, will write inequalities or equations.

Scissors; reproducible, "Fraction Cards and Comparison Symbols," for each pair or group of students.

PROCEDURE

1. Review the methods for comparing fractions, as noted in the Background, with your students. If necessary, also review the meaning of the inequality and equal symbols.

2. Distribute copies of the reproducible. Explain that it contains 18 Fraction Cards and 9 Comparison Symbol Cards. Note that the symbols are also labeled so that the inequality symbols are not inadvertently turned upside down.

3. Explain that students are to cut out the cards and use them to form six inequalities and three equations. Note that there may be several ways to do this. They must use every fraction card and each comparison symbol card, but only once.

4. Instruct your students to arrange the cards to form all six inequalities and three equations first, and then write the comparisons on a separate sheet of paper.

CLOSURE

Review the comparisons with your students. Note some of the many different comparisons that are possible. Ask for volunteers to explain what strategies they used to write their comparisons.

ANSWERS

Comparisons may vary; following are some examples. **(1)** $\frac{1}{2} < \frac{2}{3}$ **(2)** $\frac{4}{5} = \frac{8}{10}$ **(3)** $\frac{7}{8} > \frac{2}{4}$ **(4)** $\frac{4}{12} = \frac{1}{3}$ **(5)** $\frac{3}{4} > \frac{2}{5}$ **(6)** $\frac{5}{6} > \frac{6}{10}$ **(7)** $\frac{10}{100} = \frac{1}{10}$ **(8)** $\frac{5}{12} < \frac{3}{6}$ **(9)** $\frac{1}{5} < \frac{7}{10}$

FRACTION CARDS AND COMPARISON SYMBOLS

Fraction Cards

$\dfrac{1}{2}$	$\dfrac{5}{6}$	$\dfrac{7}{8}$
$\dfrac{1}{3}$	$\dfrac{2}{3}$	$\dfrac{3}{6}$
$\dfrac{6}{10}$	$\dfrac{4}{5}$	$\dfrac{2}{4}$
$\dfrac{7}{10}$	$\dfrac{8}{10}$	$\dfrac{3}{4}$
$\dfrac{10}{100}$	$\dfrac{4}{12}$	$\dfrac{2}{5}$
$\dfrac{1}{5}$	$\dfrac{1}{10}$	$\dfrac{5}{12}$

Comparison Symbol Cards

< is less than
< is less than
< is less than
> is greater than
> is greater than
> is greater than
= is equal to
= is equal to
= is equal to

Number and Operations—Fractions: 4.NF.3

"Build fractions from unit fractions by applying and extending previous understandings of operations on whole numbers."

3. "Understand a fraction $\frac{a}{b}$ with $a > 1$ as a sum of fractions $\frac{1}{b}$.

   a. "Understand addition and subtraction of fractions as joining and separating parts referring to the same whole.

   b. "Decompose a fraction into a sum of fractions with the same denominator in more than one way, recording each decomposition by an equation. Justify decompositions, e.g., by using a visual fraction model.

   c. "Add and subtract mixed numbers with like denominators, e.g., by replacing each mixed number with an equivalent fraction, and/or by using properties of operations and the relationship between addition and subtraction.

   d. "Solve word problems involving addition and subtraction of fractions referring to the same whole and having like denominators, e.g., by using visual fraction models and equations to represent the problem."

BACKGROUND

A unit fraction is a fraction whose numerator is 1. All fractions whose numerator is larger than 1 can be expressed as either the sum of unit fractions or the sum of other fractions that have the same denominator.

For example, $\frac{4}{5}$ can be expressed as $\frac{1}{5} + \frac{1}{5} + \frac{1}{5} + \frac{1}{5}$ or $\frac{1}{5} + \frac{3}{5}$ or $\frac{2}{5} + \frac{2}{5}$.

Mixed numbers with the same denominator can be added or subtracted by adding or subtracting the numerators, then adding or subtracting the whole numbers, and then simplifying, if necessary.

For example, $1\frac{1}{5} + 2\frac{3}{5} = 3\frac{4}{5}$.

Mixed numbers with the same denominator can also be added or subtracted by replacing each mixed number with an equivalent fraction, then adding or subtracting the numerators, and then simplifying, if necessary.

For example, $1\frac{1}{5} + 2\frac{3}{5} = \frac{6}{5} + \frac{13}{5} = \frac{19}{5} = 3\frac{4}{5}$.

(*Note:* Emphasize the term *unit fraction* wherever it is used, to help students learn the terminology.)

ACTIVITY 1: DECOMPOSING A FRACTION

Students will decompose a fraction into a sum of fractions with the same denominator in six different ways.

Scissors; reproducible, "Fraction Bars," for each student.

1. Hand out copies of the reproducible. Explain that it contains several fraction bars.

2. Explain that students are to cut out all of the fraction bars. They will use the fraction bars to decompose $\frac{5}{8}$ in six different ways and will then write an equation for each way. Order does not matter, and each fraction should have the same denominator.

CLOSURE

Ask your students what strategies they used to decompose $\frac{5}{8}$. Did they use addition? Subtraction? Did they use any other methods?

ANSWERS

Following are six ways to decompose $\frac{5}{8}$. **(1)** $\frac{5}{8} = \frac{1}{8} + \frac{1}{8} + \frac{1}{8} + \frac{1}{8} + \frac{1}{8}$ **(2)** $\frac{5}{8} = \frac{1}{8} + \frac{4}{8}$ **(3)** $\frac{5}{8} = \frac{1}{8} + \frac{1}{8} + \frac{3}{8}$ **(4)** $\frac{5}{8} = \frac{1}{8} + \frac{1}{8} + \frac{1}{8} + \frac{2}{8}$ **(5)** $\frac{5}{8} = \frac{2}{8} + \frac{3}{8}$ **(6)** $\frac{5}{8} = \frac{1}{8} + \frac{2}{8} + \frac{2}{8}$

ACTIVITY 2: MIXED NUMBER GAME

Working in pairs or groups of three, students will play a Jeopardy-like game with mixed numbers.

MATERIALS

Reproducible, "Mixed Number Game Problems," for each pair or group of students; a stopwatch or other timepiece for the teacher. Optional: One copy of reproducibles, "Game Problem Clues, I" and "Game Problem Clues, II," for the teacher.

PROCEDURE

1. Divide your class into an even number of pairs or groups of three. Arrange them in sets of two so that each pair or group can check another's answers.

2. Distribute copies of the reproducible to your students. Explain that they will play a game that is similar to Jeopardy, but with some differences. Instead of a board, they have a paper with the answers to problems across the top and boxes under each answer,

numbered 1–4, in which students are to write problems for each answer. You might suggest that students use scratch paper to write down clues and work out problems.

3. Explain the procedure of the game. A student selects an answer and a box and then you will read a clue, for example from "Game Problem Clues, I" for Box 1 under the answer $3\frac{7}{10}$. The clue will help students to write a problem that will result in the correct answer. Depending on your students, you might find it helpful to write the first problem together as a class. Explain that after you read the clue, students will have 30 seconds to confer with their partners and write the correct problem in the box by the number beneath the answer. (You may adjust the time depending on the needs of your students.) At the end of 30 seconds, each pair or group of students will exchange their paper with the pair or group with whom they are working. When you announce the correct problem, students will mark whether the problem is correct or not. A correct problem for each answer is included after each clue. Answers may vary slightly. For example, for the first answer, first clue, students may provide problems of $1\frac{3}{10} + 2\frac{4}{10}$ or $1\frac{4}{10} + 2\frac{3}{10}$. Problems such as $2\frac{3}{10} + 1\frac{4}{10}$ or $2\frac{4}{10} + 1\frac{3}{10}$ are also correct. Tell your students that correct problems receive one point. After correcting the problems, students hand the papers back to their owners and you will call on a student to select the next answer. The student will say the answer he chooses and the box number and the game continues.

4. Tell your students that for each answer two boxes will contain addition problems, and two boxes will contain subtraction problems. Explain that you will say the clue once, pause, and then repeat it. You will then say "Start," and keep time. When the time limit is up, announce "time's up." Pairs and groups will exchange their papers and you will announce the correct problem. Because answers may take slightly different forms, ask your students for other possible correct problems.

5. Have a student select the first answer and box and start the game.

CLOSURE

Tally scores and announce the pairs or groups with the most points. Discuss any answers and clues that students had trouble with.

 ACTIVITY 3: PROBLEMS, MODELS, AND EQUATIONS

Working in groups, students will solve word problems with fractions with like denominators, create models of the problems, and write equations to represent the problems.

MATERIALS

Rulers; markers; crayons; colored pencils; drawing paper; reproducible, "Fraction Word Problems," for each group.

1. Review adding and subtracting fractions with like denominators: Add the numerators and write the sum over the original denominator. Provide examples such as the following.

   - $\frac{1}{4} + \frac{2}{4} = \frac{3}{4}$

   - $\frac{3}{5} - \frac{2}{5} = \frac{1}{5}$

   - $\frac{2}{3} + \frac{2}{3} = \frac{4}{3} = 1\frac{1}{3}$ (Remind students that they must simplify, if necessary.)

2. Provide an example of a fraction model, such as the one below that models $\frac{1}{3} + \frac{1}{3} = \frac{2}{3}$.

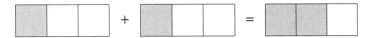

3. Hand out copies of the reproducible and explain that it contains three word problems involving addition and subtraction of fractions with like denominators.

4. Assign either the first two problems, or all three. Note that the third problem, designated by "A Challenge," requires addition and subtraction.

5. Explain that students are to first solve the problems. Then, using drawing paper, they will create a visual fraction model of each problem. They are also to write an equation that represents the problem beneath each problem.

CLOSURE

Discuss students' work. Review any answers, models, or equations that they found to be difficult. Display the models.

ANSWERS

The answer is followed by a description of a possible model and an equation. **(1)** $\frac{5}{8}$ A circle is divided into 8 equal pieces. 5 of the pieces are shaded. $\frac{3}{8} + \frac{2}{8} = \frac{5}{8}$ **(2)** $\frac{2}{4}$ or $\frac{1}{2}$ A whole is divided into 4 equal parts. 3 of the parts are shaded. 1 of the shaded parts is taken away. 2 shaded parts remain. $\frac{3}{4} - \frac{1}{4} = \frac{2}{4} = \frac{1}{2}$ **(3)** $\frac{1}{5}$ A whole is divided into 5 parts. 4 of the parts are shaded, representing the part of the class that wore either a red, white, or blue shirt. 1 of the 5 parts represents the fraction of students who wore white shirts. 2 of the 5 parts represent the fraction of students who wore blue shirts. 1 of 5 parts represents the fraction of the class that wore red shirts. $\frac{4}{5} - \left(\frac{1}{5} + \frac{2}{5}\right) = \frac{1}{5}$

1

$\frac{1}{8}$	$\frac{1}{8}$	$\frac{1}{8}$	$\frac{1}{8}$	$\frac{1}{8}$	$\frac{1}{8}$	$\frac{1}{8}$	$\frac{1}{8}$
$\frac{1}{8}$	$\frac{1}{8}$	$\frac{1}{8}$	$\frac{1}{8}$	$\frac{1}{8}$	$\frac{1}{8}$	$\frac{1}{8}$	$\frac{1}{8}$

$\frac{2}{8}$	$\frac{2}{8}$	$\frac{2}{8}$	$\frac{2}{8}$

$\frac{3}{8}$	$\frac{3}{8}$

$\frac{4}{8}$	$\frac{4}{8}$

$\frac{5}{8}$

Name _____ Date _____

MIXED NUMBER GAME PROBLEMS

$3\frac{7}{10}$	$2\frac{3}{8}$	$4\frac{2}{5}$	$6\frac{5}{12}$
1.	1.	1.	1.
2.	2.	2.	2.
3.	3.	3.	3.
4.	4.	4.	4.

Answer $3\frac{7}{10}$	Clues	Problems
Box 1.	This is an addition problem. There are two mixed numbers and one numerator is 3.	$1\frac{3}{10} + 2\frac{4}{10}$
Box 2.	This is a subtraction problem. One mixed number has two 2s.	$5\frac{9}{10} - 2\frac{2}{10}$
Box 3.	This is an addition problem. It has one whole number and one fraction.	$3 + \frac{7}{10}$
Box 4.	This is a subtraction problem. It has one mixed number and one unit fraction.	$3\frac{8}{10} - \frac{1}{10}$

Answer $2\frac{3}{8}$	Clues	Problems
Box 1.	This is a subtraction problem. One of the mixed numbers has a 6 and a numerator of 5.	$6\frac{5}{8} - 4\frac{2}{8}$
Box 2.	This is a subtraction problem. One of the mixed numbers has a 2 and a numerator of 4.	$4\frac{7}{8} - 2\frac{4}{8}$
Box 3.	This is an addition problem. It has a whole number and a mixed number.	$1 + 1\frac{3}{8}$
Box 4.	This is an addition problem. It has a mixed number and a unit fraction.	$2\frac{2}{8} + \frac{1}{8}$

Answer $4\frac{2}{5}$	Clues	Problems
Box 1.	This is an addition problem. One of the addends is zero.	$4\frac{2}{5} + 0$
Box 2.	This is a subtraction problem. One of the mixed numbers has an 8 and a numerator of 4.	$8\frac{4}{5} - 4\frac{2}{5}$
Box 3.	This is a subtraction problem. The mixed number has an 8 and there is only one numerator in the problem.	$8\frac{2}{5} - 4$
Box 4.	This is an addition problem. There are two mixed numbers. One of the mixed numbers has two 1s.	$1\frac{1}{5} + 3\frac{1}{5}$

Answer $6\frac{5}{12}$	Clues	Problems
Box 1.	This is an addition problem. It has one whole number and one fraction.	$6 + \frac{5}{12}$
Box 2.	This is an addition problem. One of the mixed numbers has a 4 and a numerator of 2.	$4\frac{2}{12} + 2\frac{3}{12}$
Box 3.	This is a subtraction problem. One of the mixed numbers has two 4s.	$10\frac{9}{12} - 4\frac{4}{12}$
Box 4.	This is a subtraction problem. One of the mixed numbers has a 12 that is not a denominator and the other mixed number has a numerator of 5.	$12\frac{10}{12} - 6\frac{5}{12}$

FRACTION WORD PROBLEMS

Directions: Solve each problem. Then create a model of the problem that shows your solution. Under each model, write an equation that represents the problem.

1. Jason and his mom had pizza for dinner. The pie was cut into 8 equal-sized slices. Jason ate 3 slices and his mom ate 2 slices. How much of the pie did they eat?

2. Liz was helping her mother bake cookies. She had $\frac{3}{4}$ of a cup of sugar. The recipe called for $\frac{1}{4}$ of a cup. How much sugar was left over?

A Challenge

3. On flag day, $\frac{4}{5}$ of Deena's class wore either a red, a white, or a blue shirt. $\frac{1}{5}$ of the class wore white shirts. $\frac{2}{5}$ wore blue shirts. What fraction of the class wore red shirts?

Number and Operations—Fractions: 4.NF.4

"Build fractions from unit fractions by applying and extending previous understandings of operations on whole numbers."

4. "Apply and extend previous understandings of multiplication to multiply a fraction by a whole number.

    a. "Understand a fraction $\frac{a}{b}$ as a multiple of $\frac{1}{b}$.

    b. "Understand a multiple of $\frac{a}{b}$ as a multiple of $\frac{1}{b}$, and use this understanding to multiply a fraction by a whole number.

    c. "Solve word problems involving multiplication of a fraction by a whole number, e.g., by using visual fraction models and equations to represent the problem."

BACKGROUND

Multiplication of a fraction by a whole number requires students to multiply the numerator of the fraction by the whole number. For example, $3 \times \frac{1}{4}$ can be modeled by 3 groups of 4 equal parts with 1 out of the 4 equal parts shaded in each group.

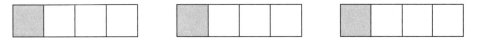

The product can be expressed as $3 \times \frac{1}{4} = \frac{3}{4}$.

Here is another example: $5 \times \frac{3}{4}$ can be modeled by 5 groups of 4 equal parts with 3 out of the 4 parts shaded in each group.

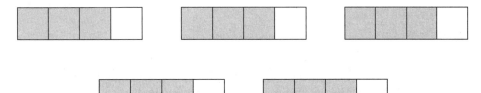

The product can be expressed as $5 \times \frac{3}{4} = \frac{15}{4} = 3\frac{3}{4}$. Using a unit fraction, the product can be expressed as $15 \times \frac{1}{4} = \frac{15}{4} = 3\frac{3}{4}$.

ACTIVITY: COMPLETE THE ROWS

Working in groups, students will cut out cards and arrange them so that a word problem, its visual fraction model, the equation that represents the problem, and the answer are in a row.

MATERIALS

Scissors; glue sticks; construction paper; reproducible, "Completion Cards," for each group.

PROCEDURE

1. Hand out copies of the reproducible. Explain that it contains four columns of cards: Word Problems, Models, Equations, and Answers. There are a total of 24 cards.

2. Explain that each word problem can be solved by using a visual fraction model and one or two different equations.

3. Instruct students to cut out the cards. Starting with the first word problem, they should find the visual fraction model and equation, or equivalent equation, that can be used to solve the problem. Then they should find the answer to the problem.

4. Explain that after finding the solution to a problem, students should glue the problem, model, equation or equations, and the answer in a row on their construction paper. They are to do this for all five problems. Note that no cards should be left over and no card can be used more than once.

CLOSURE

Discuss students' work and the strategies they used to match problems, models, equations, and answers. Review any problems that proved to be difficult.

ANSWERS

Cards are arranged in a row. **Row 1:** 1, 7, 14, 19, 20 **Row 2:** 2, 9, 12, 18, 24
Row 3: 3, 10, 13, 22 **Row 4:** 4, 8, 15, 17, 21 **Row 5:** 5, 6, 11, 16, 23

COMPLETION CARDS

Word Problems	Models	Equations	Answers
1. Mike has 2 coupons. Each is worth $\frac{3}{4}$ of a dollar. What is the total value of the coupons?	**6.**	**11.** $6 \times \frac{1}{3} = n$	**20.** $n = 1\frac{1}{2}$
		12. $2 \times \frac{2}{5} = n$	
2. Rui studied his vocabulary words for two nights. Each night, he learned $\frac{2}{5}$ of the words on the list. After the second night, what part of the words did he know?	**7.**	**13.** $2 \times \frac{1}{4} = n$	**21.** $n = 1\frac{1}{4}$
		14. $2 \times \frac{3}{4} = n$	
3. Sally made two batches of cookies. Each required $\frac{1}{4}$ cup of small candies. How many cups of candies did she need?	**8.**	**15.** $2 \times \frac{5}{8} = n$	**22.** $n = \frac{1}{2}$
		16. $3 \times \frac{2}{3} = n$	
4. Linda made 2 bowls of punch. She needed $\frac{5}{8}$ of a gallon of juice for each bowl. How much juice did she need?	**9.**	**17.** $10 \times \frac{1}{8} = n$	**23.** $n = 2$
		18. $4 \times \frac{1}{5} = n$	
5. Sam has a recipe for cookies, which calls for $\frac{2}{3}$ cup of sugar. He is tripling the recipe. How much sugar does he need?	**10.**	**19.** $6 \times \frac{1}{4} = n$	**24.** $n = \frac{4}{5}$

Number and Operations—Fractions: 4.NF.5

"Understand decimal notation for fractions, and compare decimal fractions."

> 5. "Express a fraction with denominator 10 as an equivalent fraction with denominator 100, and use this technique to add two fractions with respective denominators 10 and 100."

BACKGROUND

To express a fraction with a denominator of 10 as an equivalent fraction with a denominator of 100, students should use the multiplication property of one, which states that any number multiplied by 1 equals the number.

1 can be expressed as $\frac{10}{10}$. Multiplying a fraction with a denominator of 10 by $\frac{10}{10}$ will result in an equivalent fraction with a denominator of 100. For example, $\frac{7}{10} \times \frac{10}{10} = \frac{70}{100}$.

To add fractions with denominators of 10 and 100, students should write an equivalent fraction that has a denominator of 100 and then add the fractions. For example, $\frac{7}{10} + \frac{8}{100} = \frac{70}{100} + \frac{8}{100} = \frac{78}{100}$.

ACTIVITY: FRACTION BINGO

Students will create a fraction bingo board by writing fractions from the Fraction Bank in each square on the board. You will present fraction problems, which students will solve. If the answer is on the student's board, the student will use a counter to cover the square that contains the answer. The first student to cover five squares in a row, column, or diagonal is the winner.

MATERIALS

24 1-inch diameter (or smaller) counters; reproducible, "Fraction Bingo," for each student. Optional: One copy of reproducible, "Fraction Problem Bank," for the teacher.

PROCEDURE

1. Distribute copies of the Fraction Bingo board reproducible to your students.

2. Explain that students are to randomly fill in each square on their board with a number from the Fraction Bank. They should not fill in the free space with a number. As they fill in a number, suggest that they cross out the number in the Fraction Bank so that they will not use the same number twice. Note that all numbers will be used.

3. Explain the rules of the game. You will present problems in order, starting with number 1 on the "Fraction Problem Bank." (*Note:* You may make a copy of the problem bank or

simply read the problems from the page in your book.) Explain that after you present a problem, students are to solve the problem. Provide a few moments for them to work out the answer. They may use scratch paper. If they are correct, the answer will be on their board. Students who find the answer to the problem on their board should place a counter on the number. (*Note:* Having students use counters, instead of marking on the paper, allows you to use the same bingo boards for additional rounds of the game. Should you decide to play another round, present the problems in a different order.) Continue presenting problems until a student gets bingo by covering five squares in a row, column, or diagonal with counters.

4. After a student announces she has bingo, check her answers to make sure that she is correct.

CLOSURE

Announce all the correct answers and allow other students to make certain that their answers are correct. Review any problems that students found confusing.

ANSWERS

(1) $\frac{30}{100}$ (2) $\frac{52}{100}$ (3) $\frac{38}{100}$ (4) $\frac{21}{100}$ (5) $\frac{12}{100}$ (6) $\frac{61}{100}$ (7) $\frac{88}{100}$ (8) $\frac{16}{100}$ (9) $\frac{20}{100}$ (10) $\frac{50}{100}$ (11) $\frac{35}{100}$ (12) $\frac{4}{10}$

(13) $\frac{45}{100}$ (14) $\frac{13}{100}$ (15) $\frac{84}{100}$ (16) $\frac{87}{100}$ (17) $\frac{54}{100}$ (18) $\frac{64}{100}$ (19) $\frac{97}{100}$ (20) $\frac{31}{100}$ (21) $\frac{7}{10}$ (22) $\frac{80}{100}$

(23) $\frac{58}{100}$ (24) $\frac{96}{100}$

FRACTION BINGO

		Free Space		

Fraction Bank

$\frac{4}{10}$	$\frac{7}{10}$	$\frac{12}{100}$	$\frac{13}{100}$	$\frac{16}{100}$	$\frac{20}{100}$
$\frac{21}{100}$	$\frac{30}{100}$	$\frac{31}{100}$	$\frac{35}{100}$	$\frac{38}{100}$	$\frac{45}{100}$
$\frac{50}{100}$	$\frac{52}{100}$	$\frac{54}{100}$	$\frac{58}{100}$	$\frac{61}{100}$	$\frac{64}{100}$
$\frac{80}{100}$	$\frac{84}{100}$	$\frac{87}{100}$	$\frac{88}{100}$	$\frac{96}{100}$	$\frac{97}{100}$

FRACTION PROBLEM BANK

1. $\frac{3}{10} = ?$	2. $\frac{5}{10} + \frac{2}{100} = ?$	3. $\frac{3}{10} + \frac{8}{100} = ?$	4. $\frac{2}{10} + \frac{1}{100} = ?$
5. $\frac{1}{10} + \frac{2}{100} = ?$	6. $\frac{6}{10} + \frac{1}{100} = ?$	7. $\frac{8}{10} + \frac{8}{100} = ?$	8. $\frac{1}{10} + \frac{6}{100} = ?$
9. $\frac{1}{10} + \frac{10}{100} = ?$	10. $\frac{5}{10} = ?$	11. $\frac{3}{10} + \frac{5}{100} = ?$	12. $\frac{40}{100} = ?$
13. $\frac{4}{10} + \frac{5}{100} = ?$	14. $\frac{1}{10} + \frac{3}{100} = ?$	15. $\frac{8}{10} + \frac{4}{100} = ?$	16. $\frac{8}{10} + \frac{7}{100} = ?$
17. $\frac{5}{10} + \frac{4}{100} = ?$	18. $\frac{6}{10} + \frac{4}{100} = ?$	19. $\frac{9}{10} + \frac{7}{100} = ?$	20. $\frac{3}{10} + \frac{1}{100} = ?$
21. $\frac{70}{100} = ?$	22. $\frac{8}{10} = ?$	23. $\frac{5}{10} + \frac{8}{100} = ?$	24. $\frac{9}{10} + \frac{6}{100} = ?$

Number and Operations—Fractions: 4.NF.6

"Understand decimal notation for fractions, and compare decimal fractions."

> 6. "Use decimal notation for fractions with denominators 10 or 100."

BACKGROUND

To write a decimal for fractions with denominators of 10 or 100, students must be able to read the fraction and insert the digits in their proper places according to place value.

- $\frac{8}{10}$ is read "8 tenths" and equals 0.8.

- $\frac{27}{100}$ is read "27 hundredths" and equals 0.27.

- $3\frac{19}{100}$ is read "3 and 19 hundredths" and equals 3.19. Note that the *and* in "3 and 19 hundredths" represents the decimal point.

ACTIVITY 1: MATCHING FRACTIONS AND DECIMALS

Students will match a decimal with its equivalent fraction by arranging triangles, placing equivalent values on adjacent sides.

MATERIALS

Scissors; reproducibles, "Fraction Triangles, I" and "Fraction Triangles, II," for each student.

PROCEDURE

1. Explain that every fraction can be written as an equivalent decimal. Provide examples, such as the following:

$$\frac{9}{10} = 0.9 \qquad \frac{21}{100} = 0.21 \qquad 1\frac{89}{100} = 1.89$$

2. Distribute copies of the reproducibles. Explain that each reproducible has six triangles, which are identified by a circled number. Each side of every triangle has a fraction or a decimal. The 12 triangles can be arranged in a manner so that every fraction is paired with an equivalent decimal on sides that are next to each other. Note that some fractions or decimals will not have equivalent values on other triangles.

3. Instruct your students to cut out the triangles and arrange them so that equivalent values are next to each other on adjacent sides of the triangles.

Discuss the arrangement of the triangles and the strategies students used to match equivalent fractions and decimals.

ANSWERS

The number of each triangle is provided and indicates the triangle's position. By arranging the triangles in this manner, equivalent fractions and decimals will be on adjacent sides.

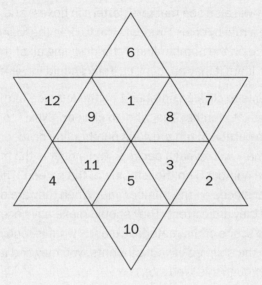

ACTIVITY 2: LOCATING DECIMALS ON A NUMBER LINE

Working in pairs or groups of three, students will visit a Web site and virtually locate decimals on a number line.

MATERIALS

Computers with Internet access for students; computer with Internet access and digital projector for the teacher.

PROCEDURE

1. Instruct your students to go to www.mymaths.co.uk/samples/decimalLines.html. Explain that students will be working with decimal values and a number line.

2. Instruct them to click on number 1 on the left side of the screen. Students will see a number line ranging from 0 to 10. They should click on "Next" at the bottom left of the screen.

Below the first number line they will now see a second number line with question marks. Each question mark represents a decimal. These decimals are located between the two numbers that the magnifying glass focuses on. Students should click on all of the question marks to reveal the values of the decimals.

3. Instruct your students to click on number 2 on the left side of the screen. They will see a number line with decimals below it. Students are to drag the given numbers to their correct places. When they are finished, they should click on "Markit," at the lower right of the screen. They will learn if they placed the decimals correctly; they should correct any decimals that they placed incorrectly.

4. Tell your students to click on number 3 on the left side of the screen. Again, they will see a number line. They will also see markers (letters in boxes) and rules (in a box). The markers are matched to a rule by color. Students are to drag the markers according to the rules to their correct place on the number line. After dragging all of the markers, they should click on "Markit" to learn if they are correct. They should make any necessary corrections.

5. Instruct your students to click on number 4 on the left side of the screen. They will see a number line, divided into tenths. They should click on "Next" to reveal a second number line, which shows a portion of the previous number line divided into hundredths. Clicking on each question mark will reveal a decimal with a digit in the hundredths place. Tell your students to click on number 5 on the left side of the screen. They are to drag the numbers to their correct places on the number line. When they are done, they should click on "Markit" to learn if they are correct. They should make any necessary corrections. (*Note:* After number 5, the scope of the material exceeds what is required by this Standard. However, depending on the abilities of your students, you may find it worthwhile to have them continue working through this Web site.)

CLOSURE

Ask students to write an exit card explaining how to locate a decimal on a number line. Collect the exit cards. You may wish to share exceptional responses or clear up any misconceptions the next day.

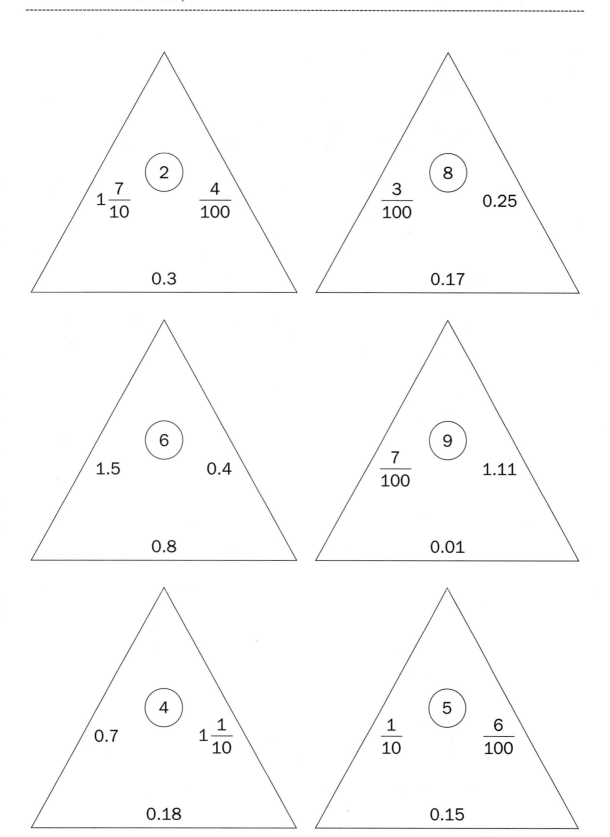

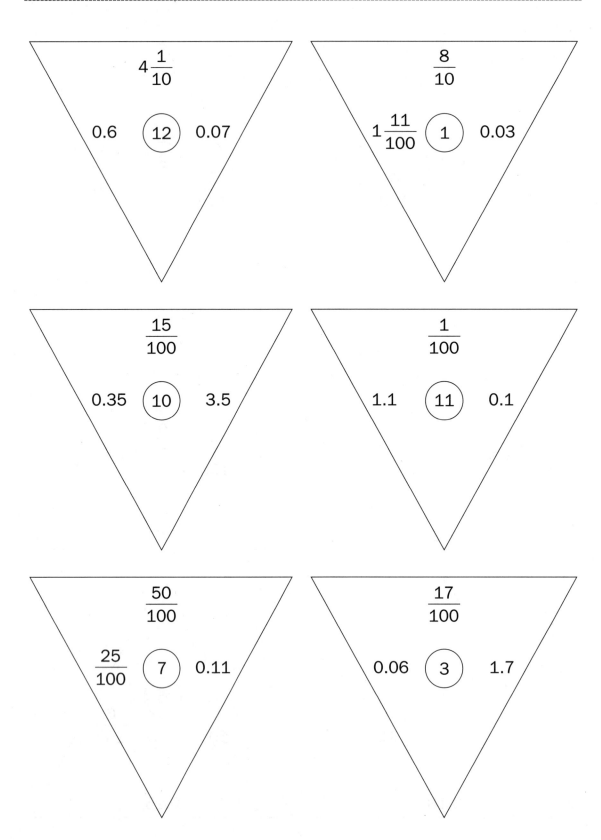

Number and Operations—Fractions: 4.NF.7

"Understand decimal notation for fractions, and compare decimal fractions."

> 7. "Compare two decimals to hundredths by reasoning about their size. Recognize that comparisons are valid only when the two decimals refer to the same whole. Record the results of comparisons with the symbols >, =, or <, and justify the conclusions, e.g., by using a visual model."

BACKGROUND

There are three ways students can compare decimals: using place value, using the number line, or making a model on graph paper.

To use place value for comparing decimals, students should compare the digits place by place. For example, to compare 0.24 and 0.3, start with the ones place. The ones are both 0. Go to the tenths place. In the first decimal there are 2 tenths, but in the second decimal there are 3 tenths. Because 3 tenths is larger than 2 tenths, 0.24 < 0.3. It does not matter that there are more digits in 0.24 because the 4 represents hundredths. If a placeholder were added in the hundredths place for 3 tenths, the decimal would be 30 hundredths. In this case it is easy to see that 0.24 < 0.30.

To use the number line to compare decimals, students should compare the positions of the decimals. The larger number is located to the right of the smaller number.

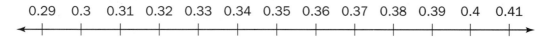

For example, to compare 0.4 and 0.38, locate their positions on the number line. Because 0.4 is to the right of 0.38, 0.4 > 0.38.

To compare 0.36 and 0.4 on graph paper, consider the model below. Note that 0.4 equals 0.40; therefore 0.36 < 0.4.

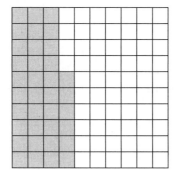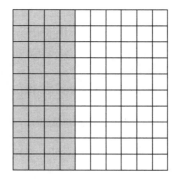

ACTIVITY: DECIMAL BATTLE

Working in pairs or groups of three, students will play a game called "Decimal Battle." Players pick cards on which decimals are written in either tenths or hundredths. They will compare the decimals and the player with the higher decimal takes the cards. At the end of the game, the student with the most cards in each pair or group wins. Students will then sketch models of their cards on number lines or on graph paper to justify their results.

MATERIALS

Scissors; rulers; markers; crayons; colored pencils; two or three sheets of graph paper; reproducible, "Decimal Battle Cards," for each pair or group of students.

PROCEDURE

1. Hand out copies of the reproducible. Explain that it contains 24 cards on which decimals are written in either tenths or hundredths. Students are to use the cards for a "decimal battle."

2. Tell students to cut out the cards. They should shuffle them and place them face down on the desk.

3. Explain the rules: each student selects a card from the pile, one card at a time. After the students have each selected a card, they are to compare the values of the decimals on their cards. The student whose card has the higher value takes both cards. In the case that the cards are of equal value, the two cards are set aside. Each student now selects another card and the process is repeated, with the student who has the higher card collecting both cards. Suggest that upon collecting cards, students keep the cards grouped in sets. This will make it easier to complete the next part of the activity. At the end of the game, the student who has the most cards is the winner.

4. Explain that after they have finished the game, each student is to select one pair of cards and use a number line or graph paper to sketch a visual model showing which decimal has the greater value. Students should also write an inequality that is represented by their model.

CLOSURE

Check students' models and announce the winners of the decimal battle. Allow students to share their models with others. Display the models showing the comparisons of decimals. As an extension, you may have your students reshuffle the cards and play another round.

0.28	0.99	0.88	0.98
0.7	0.6	0.9	0.65
0.34	0.8	0.37	0.59
0.62	0.5	0.1	0.35
0.70	0.14	0.10	0.42
0.58	0.18	0.81	0.24

Measurement and Data: 4.MD.1

"Solve problems involving measurement and conversion of measurements from a larger unit to a smaller unit."

> 1. "Know relative sizes of measurement units within one system of units including km, m, cm; kg, g; lb, oz; l, ml; hour, min, sec. Within a single system of measurement, express measurements in a larger unit in terms of a smaller unit. Record measurement equivalents in a two-column table."

BACKGROUND

In the United States, students should be familiar with both customary and metric units of measurement. Encourage your students to become familiar with the common units of measurement in both systems. Suggest that they refer to measurement charts, which should be included in their math textbook, whenever they are unsure of a measurement.

ACTIVITY: OUR TWO UNITS OF MEASUREMENT

This is a two-day activity. Working in groups, students will explore the relationship of two units of measures according to specific criteria, and then create a poster and present their results to the class.

MATERIALS

Scissors; rulers; markers; crayons; poster paper for each group; math texts; reference books on metric and customary measurement units for each group. Optional: Computers with Internet access.

PREPARATION

Before beginning this activity, obtain books from your school library on measurement systems and measurement units.

PROCEDURE

Day One

1. Divide your class into 10 groups. Assign each group to one of the pairs of measures below. (*Note:* For small classes, it is not necessary to assign all of the pairs of measurements.)

Group 1: kilometers and meters	Group 6: feet and inches
Group 2: meters and centimeters	Group 7: pounds and ounces
Group 3: kilograms and grams	Group 8: minutes and seconds
Group 4: liters and milliliters	Group 9: hours and minutes
Group 5: gallons and quarts	Group 10: days and hours

2. Explain that groups are to create a poster that shows the relationship of their two units of measure. They should include the following information on their posters:

- The size or amount of each unit compared to the other. For example, in terms of pounds and tons, 2,000 pounds = 1 ton.

- An example of an item that can be measured in terms of the larger unit.

- An example of an item that can be measured in terms of the smaller unit.

3. Explain that they are also to include a two-column table on their posters that shows the relationship of the two units for at least 5 rows. For example: 2,000 pounds = 1 ton, 4,000 pounds = 2 tons, 6,000 pounds = 3 tons, and so on.

4. Encourage students to find information for their posters in their math texts and reference books on measurement. You might also have students conduct research on the Internet.

5. Suggest that students brainstorm and sketch designs for their posters on a sheet of paper before beginning work on poster paper. Their posters should be attractive and informative.

6. If time permits, instruct students to start their posters.

Day Two

Provide time for students to complete their posters.

CLOSURE

Have students share their posters with the class. Discuss other examples of things that can be measured by the various units. Display the posters.

Measurement and Data: 4.MD.2

"Solve problems involving measurement and conversion of measurements from a larger unit to a smaller unit."

2. "Use the four operations to solve word problems involving distances, intervals of time, liquid volumes, masses of objects, and money, including problems involving simple fractions or decimals, and problems that require expressing measurements given in a larger unit in terms of a smaller unit. Represent measurement quantities using diagrams such as number line diagrams that feature a measurement scale."

BACKGROUND

Students need to acquire a basic understanding of measurement units. Most math texts include measurement tables, and you should encourage your students to consult the tables whenever necessary.

 ACTIVITY: WORD PROBLEMS WITH MEASUREMENT

Working in pairs or groups of three, students will solve word problems involving various measurement units. They are to select one of the problems and represent the measurement quantities in the problem on a number line diagram with a measurement scale.

MATERIALS

Rulers; markers; colored pencils; crayons; graph paper; reproducible, "Measurement Word Problems," for each pair or group of students.

PROCEDURE

1. Distribute copies of the reproducible. Explain that it contains five word problems that involve measurement. Students are to solve all five problems.

2. Explain that after your students solve the problems, they are to select one and represent the measurement quantities on a number line diagram that has a measurement scale. For example, such a diagram might have intervals of inches and half inches, hours and minutes and so on, depending on the problem. Students should create their number line diagram on graph paper with the units on their diagram representing the problem.

3. Instruct students to write their problem number and the problem's solution under their number line diagram.

CLOSURE

Check students' number line diagrams and discuss the answers to the problems. Note that number lines may vary somewhat, depending on the scales students use. Allow students to share their number lines with others.

ANSWERS

(1) 2.8 miles **(2)** 75 minutes, or 1 hour and 15 minutes **(3)** 3 cups **(4)** 400 grams
(5) 6 quarters, 3 dimes, 1 nickel

Name _____ Date _____

MEASUREMENT WORD PROBLEMS

Directions: Solve each problem. Then choose one of the problems and represent it on a number line diagram.

1. Roseanna walks for exercise. This week she walked a total of 7.6 miles. Last week she walked 4.8 miles. How much farther did she walk this week than last week?

2. Deon had a lot of homework last night. He finished his spelling homework in 15 minutes. He finished his math in 30 minutes. He finished his science in 20 minutes. And he finished his social studies in 10 minutes. How long did it take him to finish all of his homework? Write your answer in hours and minutes.

3. Paulo likes his grandmother's fruit juice punch. His grandmother's special recipe calls for $\frac{3}{4}$ cup of pineapple juice for every quart of punch. Paulo wants to make 1 gallon of punch. How many cups of pineapple juice will he need?

4. For her science project, Clarice knew that the total mass of 5 solid, equal-sized cubes was 2 kilograms. What was the mass in grams of each cube?

5. The lunch at Alexandra's school costs $1.85. Alexandra paid for lunch with 10 coins that totaled $1.85. What coins did she have?

Measurement and Data: 4.MD.3

"Solve problems involving measurement and conversion of measurements from a larger unit to a smaller unit."

3. "Apply the area and perimeter formulas for rectangles in real world and mathematical problems."

BACKGROUND

Perimeter and area are two topics that students encounter frequently in math. Perimeter is the distance around a closed plane figure. Area is the number of square units required to cover a surface.

The formula for finding the perimeter of a rectangle is $P = 2(l + w)$ or $P = 2l + 2w$, where P stands for perimeter, l stands for the length of a side of the rectangle, and w stands for its width. Perimeter is measured in linear units. If students know the perimeter of a rectangle, and they know the length of one side, they can find the length of an adjacent side by multiplying the length of the known side by 2, subtracting the product from the perimeter, and dividing the difference by 2. Understanding that opposite sides of a rectangle are congruent, students will now know the lengths of all the sides.

The formula for finding the area of a rectangle is $A = l \times w$, where A stands for the area, l stands for the length of a side, and w stands for the width. Area is measured in square units. If students understand the formula, and they know the area of a rectangle and the measure of one side, they may divide the area by the measure of the side they know to find the measure of the unknown side.

  ACTIVITY: MEASURING RECTANGLES

This is a two-day activity. Students will work in pairs or groups of three. On the first day, they will measure the lengths and widths of various rectangles in the classroom, find areas and perimeters, and record the measurements in a table. The teacher will use data of selected rectangles, and write questions that require students to find the length of an unknown side. On the second day, students will solve the problems.

MATERIALS

Rulers (with 1-inch or $\frac{1}{2}$-inch scales); yardsticks; reproducible, "Group Data Table," for each pair or group of students.

Make enough copies of the reproducible so that you may cut out a "Group Data Table" for each group.

PROCEDURE

Day One

1. Review the formulas for finding the perimeter of a rectangle and the formula for finding the area of a rectangle, as provided in the Background.

2. Explain that each pair or group of students will select three rectangles in the classroom to measure, for example: book covers, floor tiles, desks, bulletin boards, doors, windows, shelves, and computer screens.

3. Distribute a copy of the "Group Data Table" to each pair or group of students. Explain that students are to complete the table for each rectangle they measure.

4. Explain that they are to measure the length and width of their rectangles, one at a time. Suggest that they measure to the nearest inch or half inch, depending on the abilities of your students. If necessary, demonstrate how they can do this. They are to use their measurements of a rectangle to find its perimeter and area. Remind them to use correct units, for instance, square units for area. Suggest that students use the appropriate formula for finding perimeters and areas.

5. Instruct your students to hand in their completed tables at the end of class.

6. Before the next class, use the information from students' tables to develop questions. Try to develop one or two questions based on one rectangle for each pair or group of students. One question could relate to area and the other could be about perimeter. Here are two examples: Group 1 [or you may prefer to name the students] said that this book's cover is 9 inches long and has an area of 54 square inches. What is the cover's width? Given that the perimeter of a rectangle is 40 inches, and the length of a side is 12 inches, what is the length of the opposite side?

Day Two

1. Ask students the questions you developed. (*Note:* Students who measured a particular rectangle should refrain from answering questions about it.)

2. Whenever possible, hold up or stand next to a rectangle to help students visualize the dimensions.

Ask students to write exit cards that explain how to find a missing side if they are given the area and length of one side of a rectangle. Ask students to explain how to find a missing side of a rectangle if they are given the perimeter and the length of a side.

You might also ask your students questions, such as the following:

- Which formula for finding the perimeter of a rectangle, $P = 2(l + w)$ or $P = 2l + 2w$, do you find easier to work with? Why?

- What is meant by the term "square unit"?

GROUP DATA TABLE

Names _____

Rectangle that was measured	Location	Length	Width	Area	Perimeter

Names _____

Rectangle that was measured	Location	Length	Width	Area	Perimeter

Measurement and Data: 4.MD.4

"Represent and interpret data."

> 4. "Make a line plot to display a data set of measurements in fractions of a unit $\left(\frac{1}{2}, \frac{1}{4}, \frac{1}{8}\right)$. Solve problems involving addition and subtraction of fractions by using information presented in line plots."

BACKGROUND

A line plot, also known as a dot plot, displays data along a number line. Each value of the data is marked with a symbol noting the frequency.

For example, a line plot displaying the lengths $5\frac{3}{8}, 6\frac{5}{8}, 7\frac{1}{8}, 7\frac{1}{2},$ and $7\frac{1}{2}$ is shown below.

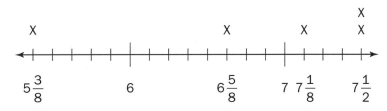

Note that an X is placed above the value each time the value appears.

ACTIVITY: PENCILS AND LINE PLOTS

Students will measure their pencils and draw a line plot that shows this data.

MATERIALS

Ruler with a $\frac{1}{8}$ -inch scale; a pencil; reproducible, "Pencil Lengths," for each student. (*Note:* Pencils should be of various lengths.)

PROCEDURE

1. Explain that students will make a line plot of pencil lengths. Explain what a line plot is and offer the example provided in the Background.

2. Hand out copies of the reproducible. Explain that it has three columns in which there are spaces for the measurements of 30 students' pencils. There is also a line at the bottom of the sheet that will serve as a line plot that students will complete.

3. Explain that students are to measure their pencils, using a ruler with a $\frac{1}{8}$-inch scale. If necessary, demonstrate how students can find the length of their pencil using the ruler.

   - Explain that they must align the end of the pencil with the first tick mark on the ruler.

   - Note that inches are represented by whole numbers. One tick mark to the right represents $\frac{1}{8}$ of an inch. Two tick marks represent $\frac{2}{8}$ or $\frac{1}{4}$ of an inch. For example, 4 tick marks to the right of 6 is $6\frac{4}{8}$ or $6\frac{1}{2}$ inches.

4. Call the name of the first student in your grade book. Ask for the length of his or her pencil. Students are to record this length in the space next to Student 1 on the reproducible. You may find it helpful to also record this information on the board.

5. Continue calling on students, in order according to your grade book, until all students have provided the length of their pencils.

6. Explain how students can construct their line plot.

   - Find the smallest and largest values. In this case, these are the shortest and longest pencil lengths.

   - Place a small vertical line near the left on the horizontal line at the bottom of the reproducible to represent the smallest pencil length.

   - Using a ruler and starting with the smallest value, mark the line at $\frac{1}{8}$-inch intervals, stopping at the number that represents the longest pencil length.

   - Place an X every time a value is given. Label the line plot at 1-inch intervals.

7. Instruct your students to use their completed line plots to write an addition or subtraction problem that can be solved using their line plot. For example: What is the sum of the lengths of the three smallest pencils? What is the difference between the shortest and longest pencils?

8. Ask for volunteers to read their questions. The other students should solve the problems.

CLOSURE

Discuss students' line plots. Ask how the line plots made it easier to solve the problems that students wrote.

Name _____ Date _____

PENCIL LENGTHS

Student	Pencil Length
1	
2	
3	
4	
5	
6	
7	
8	
9	
10	

Student	Pencil Length
11	
12	
13	
14	
15	
16	
17	
18	
19	
20	

Student	Pencil Length
21	
22	
23	
24	
25	
26	
27	
28	
29	
30	

Pencil Lengths

Measurement and Data: 4.MD.5

"Geometric measurement: understand concepts of angle and measure angles."

5. "Recognize angles as geometric shapes that are formed wherever two rays share a common endpoint, and understand concepts of angle measurement:

a. "An angle is measured with reference to a circle with its center at the common endpoint of the rays, by considering the fraction of the circular arc between the points where the two rays intersect the circle. An angle that turns through $\frac{1}{360}$ of a circle is called a 'one-degree angle,' and can be used to measure angles.

b. "An angle that turns through n one-degree angles is said to have an angle measure of n degrees."

BACKGROUND

An angle is a geometric figure formed by two rays with a common endpoint. This endpoint is called the vertex of the angle. Angles are measured in degrees. If the vertex of an angle is placed at the center of a circle, and the circle is divided into 360 pie-shaped regions, the angle formed by two adjacent rays is 1°.

ACTIVITY: MAKING AN ANGLE

Students will make a model of an angle by cutting out two rays and attaching them with a paper fastener.

MATERIALS

Scissors; protractor; card stock; 1 round-top paper fastener; reproducible, "Rays," for each student; hole punchers that students will share.

PREPARATION

Copy the reproducible on card stock.

PROCEDURE

1. Explain that an angle is formed by two rays that have the same endpoint. If necessary, draw an angle on the board and note the rays and the vertex. Tell students that they will make a model of an angle.

2. Distribute copies of the reproducible. Explain that it contains two arrows, which represent the sides of the angle.

3. Instruct students to cut out the arrows.

4. After students have cut out their arrows, explain that there should be a small circle at the end of each arrow. Students are to use a hole punch to punch out the circles.

5. After students have punched out the small circles, instruct them to place the arrows, one on top of the other with the small holes aligned. They should place the end of the paper fastener through both holes so that the round end of the fastener is on top of the top arrow, and then open the bottom of the fastener and fold it up.

6. Explain that the point where the sides of their arrows are joined represents the vertex of the angle. The arrows represent the sides (or rays) of the angle. The rays should be able to rotate.

7. Instruct your students to place the bottom arrow on their desk, parallel to the edge of the desk. (Having the bottom arrow aligned in this manner will help them to more easily recognize angle sizes.) Suggest that they rotate the top arrow, which represents a side of the angle, by moving it in a counterclockwise direction. (If necessary, explain that a counterclockwise direction is the opposite direction of the way the hands of a clock turn.) Students should see that the angle becomes larger. If they rotate the top arrow completely around, it will eventually coincide with the bottom arrow. Because a circle contains 360°, the angle rotated 360°. Note that a 1° angle is $\frac{1}{360}$ of the rotation. Ask your students to make a 1° angle. Students will likely be surprised at how small this angle is and how difficult it is to measure.

8. Ask students to use their angle to form a 30° angle, a 45° angle, a 60° angle, and a 90° angle. Students should verify their measurements with a protractor.

CLOSURE

Ask students to write an exit card explaining how they formed various angles.

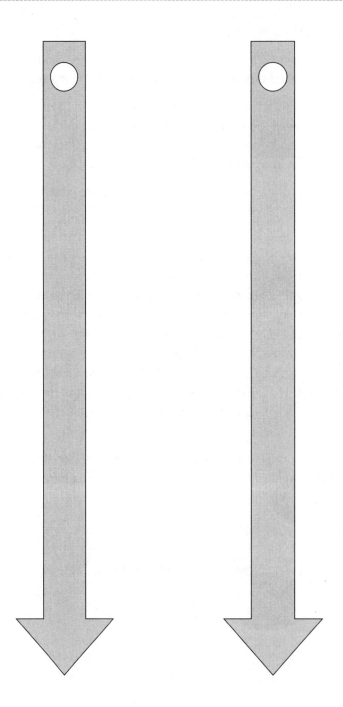

Measurement and Data: 4.MD.6

"Geometric measurement: understand concepts of angle and measure angles."

> 6. "Measure angles in whole-number degrees using a protractor. Sketch angles of specified measure."

BACKGROUND

The ability to identify acute, obtuse, and right angles can help students to measure angles correctly:

- An acute angle has a measure less than 90°. If an angle is smaller than the corner of a page in a book, the angle is acute.

- An obtuse angle has a measure greater than 90°. If an angle is larger than the corner of a page, the angle is obtuse.

- A right angle has a measure of 90°. The corner of a page represents a right angle.

ACTIVITY 1: MEASURING ANGLES VIRTUALLY

Students will measure angles virtually at a Web site.

MATERIALS

Computers with Internet access for students; computer with Internet access and digital projector for the teacher.

PROCEDURE

1. Explain to your students that for this activity they will measure angles with a virtual protractor at a Web site.

2. Review the meaning of acute angles (a measure of less than 90°), obtuse angles (a measure of more than 90°), and right angles (a measure of 90°). Provide some examples of these angles and ask students to identify them. Note that being able to recognize acute, obtuse, and right angles is helpful when measuring angles.

3. Instruct your students to go to www.mathplayground.com/measuringangles.html, where they will find "Measuring Angles."

4. Read the directions on the screen with your students. Note that the crossbar of the protractor is always aligned with the vertex of the angle. To measure the angle, students

must rotate the protractor by clicking and holding on "rotate" so that the 0° mark on the protractor lies on one of the rays of the angles. The other ray will intersect a scale on the protractor.

5. Explain that to find the measure of the angle, students should find the degree mark where the other ray passes through the scale. Students can check to ensure that they used the correct scale by deciding if the angle is acute or obtuse. If the angle is acute, the measure of the angle should be less than 90°. If the angle is obtuse, the measure of the angle should be more than 90°.

6. Demonstrate the process by clicking on "Start." Rotate your protractor so that the 0° mark on the protractor lies on one of the rays of the angle. Find the degree mark where the other ray passes through the scale. Determine if the angle is acute or obtuse to make certain you used the correct scale. Place the measure of the angle in the box by the angle symbol. Click on "Check It" and you will find if the measurement is correct.

7. Instruct your students to follow the same procedure. They will be given 10 angles to measure. If they provide an incorrect measurement, they will be given the correct measurement and should click on "Next" to measure another angle. They should also click on "Next" after correctly measuring an angle.

CLOSURE

Discuss why recognizing whether an angle is acute or obtuse is a useful strategy when measuring angles. Ask your students: Can either scale on a protractor be used easily to measure a right angle? Why?

ACTIVITY 2: ANGLE ESTIMATE AND MEASURE GAME

Working in groups of three or four, students will first estimate and draw angles with a given measure, then measure the angles to determine the accuracy of their estimated measurements.

MATERIALS

Rulers; protractors; unlined paper for each group of students.

PROCEDURE

1. If necessary, review how students can use a protractor to measure an angle.

2. Explain that students will play a game in which they must estimate, draw, and measure angles. Emphasize that the degree of the angles in the game must end in a 5 or 0 and be less than or equal to 180°. The game begins when one student in the group announces an angle of a specific degree. The other students in the group must then estimate the

size of the angle and draw it on paper with their rulers (not their protractors). When they are finished, the students must measure their angles, using their protractors. The student who announced the angle determines whose angle is closest to the actual angle. That student receives a point. If two or more students tie for the closest measure, they each receive a point. Another student of the group now announces the measurement of an angle, and the other members of the group estimate, draw, and measure it. The student with the closest angle measurement receives a point. A third student announces an angle, and the process continues with each student of the group taking turns and announcing an angle for the other group members to estimate, draw, and measure. Note that in cases where students have difficulty agreeing on the measure of an angle, you will serve as the referee.

3. The game should be played for a set time period, perhaps 15 or 20 minutes. This will give all of the students in the various groups a chance to estimate, draw, and measure several angles. You might want to mention that the more efficiently they work, the more angles they will be able to estimate, draw, and measure, and the more points they may accumulate.

CLOSURE

After time is up, declare the student with the most points in each group as the winner of his or her group. Also, determine the student who scored the most points in the class. Review the steps for measuring angles with protractors.

Measurement and Data: 4.MD.7

"Geometric measurement: understand concepts of angle and measure angles."

7. "Recognize angle measure as additive. When an angle is decomposed into non-overlapping parts, the angle measure of the whole is the sum of the angle measures of the parts. Solve addition and subtraction problems to find unknown angles on a diagram in real world and mathematical problems, e.g., by using an equation with a symbol for the unknown angle measure."

BACKGROUND

If two angles are adjacent, the sum of the measures of the two angles is equal to the measure of the large angle that is formed. This is known as the angle addition postulate, which formally states that if B is in the interior of $\angle AOC$, then the $m\angle AOB + m\angle BOC = m\angle AOC$. ($m$ is read "the measure of".)

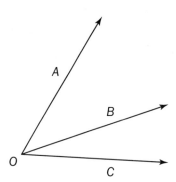

In the example above, $\angle AOB$ and $\angle BOC$ are adjacent angles.

If students know the measures of the adjacent angles, they can add the measures to find the measure of the large angle.

If students know the measure of the large angle and the measure of one adjacent angle, they can subtract to find the measure of the other adjacent angle.

 ACTIVITY: DECOMPOSING ANGLES

Working in pairs or groups of three, students will decompose three angles in different ways. They will then write an equation to express the sum of the angle measurements. They will also write equations to find missing angle measurements.

Scissors; protractors; reproducibles, "Angles" and "Angle Instruction Sheet," for each pair or group of students.

PROCEDURE

1. Explain that students will decompose (break up into two or more parts) angles into parts that do not overlap.

2. Distribute copies of reproducible, "Angles," and explain that it contains eight angles. Each one is named by a small number in the vertex. For example, the first angle is $\angle 1$.

3. Instruct your students to cut out the angles along the outside edge of the dark rays and also on the dotted lines.

4. Provide an example by instructing your students to decompose $\angle 6$ into two angles that they cut out. They should see that $\angle 5$ and $\angle 8$ can be arranged with no overlaps or gaps to fit in the interior of $\angle 6$. To show that this is true, students should measure the angles and write an equation to express the sum.

$$m\angle 6 = m\angle 5 + m\angle 8$$
$$m\angle 6 = 60°, m\angle 5 = 50°, m\angle 8 = 10°$$
$$60° = 50° + 10°$$

5. Hand out copies of reproducible, "Angle Instruction Sheet." This sheet details what students are to do. Explain that the sheet has two parts. Part I requires students to decompose the angles as in the example above. Part II requires students to write an equation for each item and find missing angle measurements that are based on descriptions. Students are to complete Parts I and II.

CLOSURE

Discuss your students' answers. Note that angles can often be decomposed in various ways. Ask students to summarize the steps for finding missing angle measurements.

ANSWERS

(1) $m\angle 1 = m\angle 5 + m\angle 4$, $80° = 50° + 30°$; $m\angle 1 = m\angle 7 + m\angle 8$, $80° = 70° + 10°$
(2) $m\angle 2 = m\angle 1 + m\angle 8$, $90° = 80° + 10°$; $m\angle 2 = m\angle 6 + m\angle 4$, $90° = 60° + 30°$
(3) $m\angle 3 = m\angle 2 + m\angle 5$, $140° = 90° + 50°$; $m\angle 3 = m\angle 6 + m\angle 1$, $140° = 60° + 80°$; $m\angle 3 = m\angle 1 + m\angle 8 + m\angle 5$, $140° = 80° + 10° + 50°$; $m\angle 3 = m\angle 6 + m\angle 7 + m\angle 8$, $140° = 60° + 70° + 10°$; $m\angle 3 = m\angle 6 + m\angle 4 + m\angle 5$, $140° = 60° + 30° + 50°$
(4) $m\angle 5 = m\angle 4 + m\angle x$, $50° = 30° + m\angle x$, $m\angle x = 20°$
(5) $m\angle 3 = m\angle 8 + m\angle y$, $140° = 10° + m\angle y$, $m\angle y = 130°$

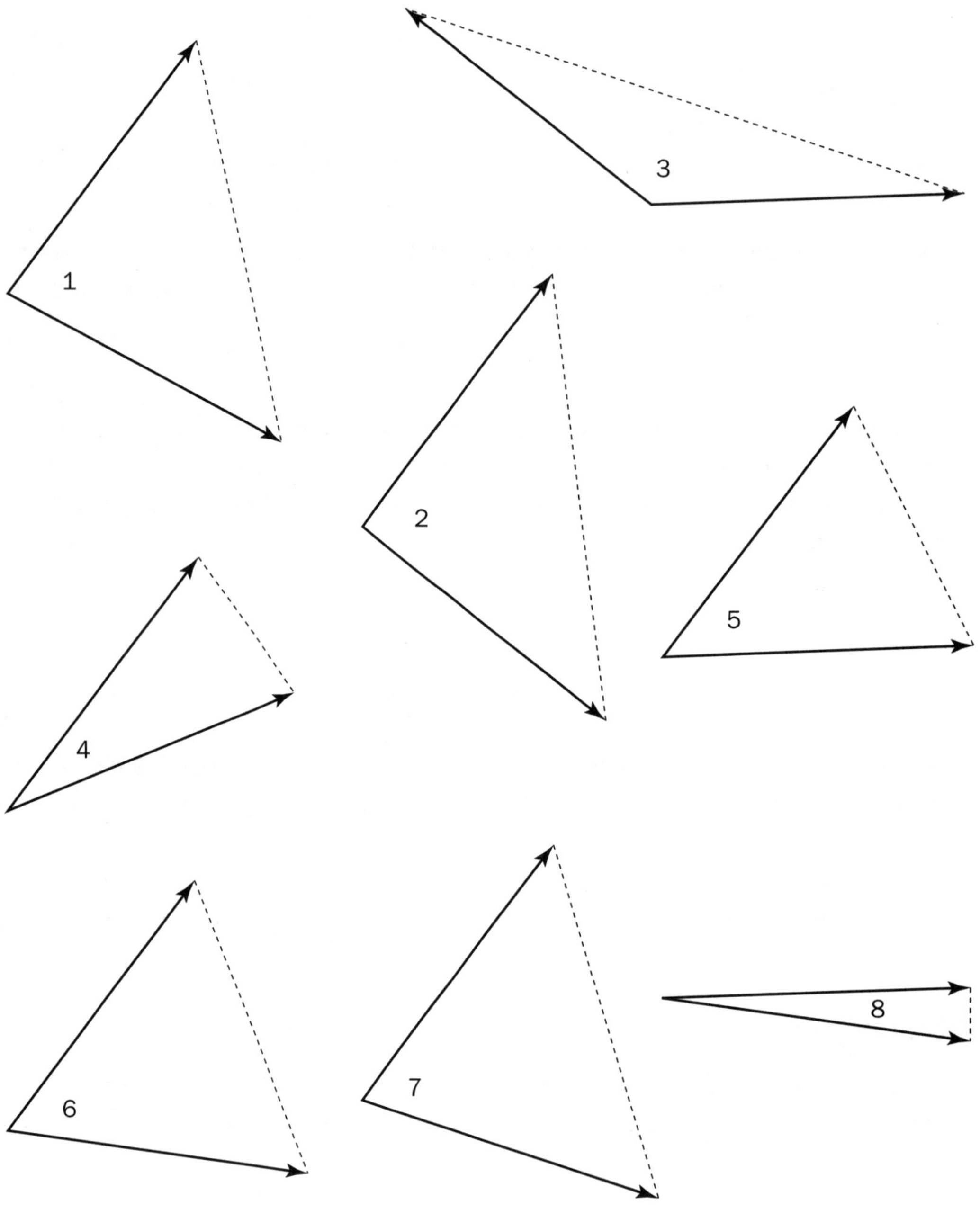
3
1
2
5
4
6
7
8

Name _____   Date _____

ANGLE INSTRUCTION SHEET

Part I: Use the angles you have cut out to decompose each angle below. Measure each angle. Then write an equation showing the sum of measures of the angles. Write your answers on this sheet.

1. Decompose ∠1 in two different ways.

2. Decompose ∠2 in two different ways.

3. Decompose ∠3 in five different ways.

Part II: Write an equation to find the unknown angle measure. Use a variable for the unknown angle measure. Then solve the equation.

4. ∠5 can be decomposed into ∠4 and another angle. The other angle is not on the "Angles" sheet. Find the measure of this missing angle.

5. ∠3 can be decomposed into ∠8 and another angle. The other angle is not on the "Angles" sheet. Find the measure of this missing angle.

163

Geometry: 4.G.1

"Draw and identify lines and angles, and classify shapes by properties of their lines and angles."

1. "Draw points, lines, line segments, rays, angles (right, acute, obtuse), and perpendicular and parallel lines. Identify these in two-dimensional figures."

BACKGROUND

As they proceed in their study of geometry, students should be familiar with basic geometric terms, such as the following:

- Point: Represented by a dot, a point is an exact location in space. It is named by a capital letter.

- Line: Extending infinitely in both directions, a line is a straight path in space. It is named by two capital letters that represent points on the line.

- Line segment: A part of a line, a line segment is named by two capital letters, each one representing an endpoint of the segment.

- Ray: A part of a line, a ray has one endpoint and is designated by two capital letters, one representing the endpoint and the other representing a point on the ray.

- Angle: An angle is a figure formed by two rays that share a common endpoint, which is the vertex of the angle. One way an angle can be named is by a capital letter that represents a point on a ray, a capital letter that represents the vertex, and a capital letter that represents a point on the other ray. Another way to name an angle is by placing a number in the vertex. A third way is to label the vertex with a capital letter.

- Perpendicular lines: Two lines are perpendicular if they are in the same plane and intersect, forming right angles.

- Parallel lines: Two lines are parallel if they are in the same plane but do not intersect. The distance between the lines remains the same.

ACTIVITY 1: DRAWING GEOMETRIC FIGURES

Students will draw points, line segments, lines, rays, angles (acute, right, and obtuse), and perpendicular and parallel lines.

MATERIALS

Ruler; protractor; unlined paper; reproducible, "Drawing Geometric Figures," for each student.

PROCEDURE

1. Explain that students will draw a variety of geometric figures. Briefly discuss the geometric figures presented in the Background and provide some examples.

2. Hand out copies of the reproducible. Explain that it contains instructions for drawing basic figures, but it does not identify the figure.

3. Tell your students to follow the instructions exactly, drawing all nine figures. They are to name and label the figures. They should use rulers and protractors to ensure accuracy.

CLOSURE

Check students' figures. Review the features of each.

ANSWERS

(1) line **(2)** acute angle **(3)** parallel lines **(4)** obtuse angle **(5)** point **(6)** ray **(7)** right angle **(8)** perpendicular lines **(9)** line segment

ACTIVITY 2: SHAPES AND STRUCTURES

Working in small groups, students will create a collage illustrating points, line segments, angles, perpendicular lines, and parallel lines.

MATERIALS

Scissors; glue sticks; markers; rulers; large construction paper; old magazines; newspapers. Optional: Computers with Internet access; printers.

PREPARATION

Prior to assigning this activity, ask students to bring in old magazines and newspapers in which they may find pictures of man-made objects and structures that provide examples of geometric figures.

PROCEDURE

1. Explain that students are to find examples of points, line segments, angles (acute, obtuse, and right), perpendicular lines, and parallel lines in pictures contained in magazines and newspapers. They should cut out the pictures and paste them onto construction paper, creating a collage. If your students have access to computers and the Internet, suggest that they go online to find and print examples of geometric figures.

2. Instruct your students to label each of the pictures in their collage. They should write the geometric figure and the object or structure it was a part of. For example: "Perpendicular lines found on a bridge" or "Right angles on windows."

3. Encourage your students to be creative, neat, and thorough with their collages. Suggest that they include more than one example of each figure to make an interesting collage.

CLOSURE

Have students share their collages with others. Display the collages.

DRAWING GEOMETRIC FIGURES

Directions: Draw, label, and name each figure.

1. Draw a line segment. Draw arrowheads at both ends of the segment. The arrowheads show that the figure extends in both directions.

2. Draw a ray. Place the crosshatch of the protractor on the endpoint of the ray. Align the ray with the 0° line on the protractor. Mark a point near the scale of the protractor to make an angle less than 90°. Draw a ray from the endpoint of the first ray through this point.

3. Draw a line. Measure an inch below one of the points on the line. Mark a point. Mark another point an inch below another point on the line. Use your ruler to connect the two points you marked. Draw arrowheads on the ends of this line segment.

4. Draw a ray. Place the crosshatch of the protractor on the endpoint of the ray. Align the ray with the 0° line on the protractor. Mark a point near the scale of the protractor to make an angle greater than 90°. Draw a ray from the endpoint of the first ray through this point.

5. Mark a dot.

6. Draw a line segment. Draw an arrowhead at the end of one endpoint of the segment.

7. Draw a ray. Place the crosshatch of the protractor on the endpoint of the ray. Align the ray with the 0° line on the protractor. Mark a point near the scale of the protractor to make an angle of 90°. Draw a ray from the endpoint of the first ray through this point.

8. Draw a line. Choose a point on the line. Place the crosshatch of the protractor on this point. Place the protractor on the line so that the 0° line of the protractor is on the line you drew. Mark a point at the 90° mark near the scale of the protractor. Use your ruler to draw a line through both points.

9. Mark two points. Use your ruler to connect the points.

Geometry: 4.G.2

"Draw and identify lines and angles, and classify shapes by properties of their lines and angles."

> 2. "Classify two-dimensional figures based on the presence or absence of parallel or perpendicular lines, or the presence or absence of angles of a specified size. Recognize right triangles as a category, and identify right triangles."

BACKGROUND

Identifying the attributes of geometric figures is an important skill. Two-dimensional figures may be classified in a variety of ways, including by the number of sides, by the measures of their angles, or whether their sides are parallel or perpendicular.

ACTIVITY: DRAWING TWO-DIMENSIONAL FIGURES

Students will draw two-dimensional figures according to their attributes.

MATERIALS

Ruler; protractor; unlined paper; reproducible, "Figures," for each student.

PROCEDURE

1. Review examples of two-dimensional figures: quadrilaterals, squares, rectangles, parallelograms, trapezoids, right triangles, acute triangles, obtuse triangles, pentagons, and hexagons. Also, review the terms: acute angle, obtuse angle, right angle, and congruent.

2. Explain that two-dimensional figures can be classified by their various attributes, such as the number of their sides, the type of their angles, and the presence of parallel or perpendicular lines.

3. Hand out copies of the reproducible. Explain that it contains attributes for nine figures. Based on the attributes, students are to draw the figures. You may also ask them to name the figures they have drawn.

4. Instruct your students to use rulers and protractors when drawing their figures. These tools will help ensure the accuracy of their drawings. If necessary, review the steps for drawing angles with a protractor.

Check the figures your students drew. Allow students to share their figures with some of their classmates. Discuss that in some cases a variety of different figures can be drawn that will share the same attributes.

ANSWERS

Student figures may vary; some attributes describe more than one figure. **(1)** Trapezoid **(2)** Rhombus **(3)** Right triangle **(4)** Obtuse triangle **(5)** Various quadrilaterals, except parallelograms, rhombuses, rectangles, and squares **(6)** Acute triangle **(7)** Rectangle, square (a square is a special kind of rectangle) **(8)** Square **(9)** Parallelogram

Directions: Draw each figure based on its attributes.

1. This quadrilateral has two parallel sides. The other two sides are not parallel.

2. This quadrilateral has four congruent sides. It has no right angles.

3. This triangle has two perpendicular sides.

4. This triangle has one obtuse angle.

5. This quadrilateral has no right angles. No sides are parallel.

6. This triangle has three acute angles.

7. This quadrilateral has four right angles.

8. This quadrilateral has four congruent sides. It has four right angles.

9. This quadrilateral has no right angles. Its opposite sides are parallel and congruent. All four sides are not congruent.

Geometry: 4.G.3

"Draw and identify lines and angles, and classify shapes by properties of their lines and angles."

> 3. "Recognize a line of symmetry for a two-dimensional figure as a line across the figure such that the figure can be folded along the line into matching parts. Identify line-symmetric figures and draw lines of symmetry."

BACKGROUND

If a figure folds along a line so that half of the figure entirely covers the other half, and the two parts are congruent, the figure has line symmetry. Following are some examples:

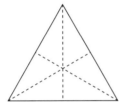 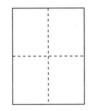

 ACTIVITY 1: LINE SYMMETRY

Students will play a game on a Web site where they will state the number of lines of symmetry of various polygons.

MATERIALS

Computers with Internet access for students; computer with Internet access and digital projector for the teacher.

PROCEDURE

1. Explain that students will play "Symmetry Game" at a Web site. They will find the number of lines of symmetry of polygons displayed on the screen.

2. Instruct your students to go to www.innovationslearning.co.uk/subjects/maths/activities /year3/symmetry/shape_game.asp. On the screen they will see the introduction to the game.

3. Demonstrate how the game works by clicking "Start." A figure will appear. Ask a volunteer how many lines of symmetry the figure has. Write that number in the white box and click

on "Enter." If the number is correct, students will see the message "Great Job," and they will receive 10 points. They should click on "Next Shape" to continue. If they are incorrect, they will see the message "So Close," and they will lose 5 points. In this case, they will see the figure folding along the lines of symmetry. After writing the correct answer, they should click on "Next Shape." Note that the game consists of 10 figures.

4. Start the game; challenge your students to score 100 points.

CLOSURE

Ask your students questions such as the following: Which of the figures had the most lines of symmetry? Which had the least? Did you find any patterns in the lines of symmetry of the various shapes? If yes, what were they? Instruct students to write a short explanation of line symmetry.

 ## ACTIVITY 2: CLASSROOM LINE SYMMETRY

Working in pairs or groups of three, students will identify two-dimensional figures in the classroom that have line symmetry.

MATERIALS

Unlined paper for sketching figures for each pair or group of students.

PROCEDURE

1. Explain that many two-dimensional figures have line symmetry. For example, a rectangular bulletin board has two lines of symmetry. Note the example of the rectangle provided in the Background.

2. Explain that students are to identify at least five two-dimensional figures in the classroom that have line symmetry. They are to sketch the figures and draw the lines of symmetry.

CLOSURE

Ask for volunteers to share their figures and the number of lines of symmetry of each with the class. Verify that students are correct.

SECTION 3

Standards and Activities for Grade 5

Operations and Algebraic Thinking: 5.OA.1

"Write and interpret numerical expressions."

1. "Use parentheses, brackets, or braces in numerical expressions, and evaluate expressions with these symbols."

BACKGROUND

The order of operations is a set of rules for evaluating expressions that contain multiple operations. It states that operations within grouping symbols must be completed before any other operations. There are several types of grouping symbols, the most common being parentheses. When evaluating expressions, operations within any grouping symbols must be completed first, followed by multiplication *or* division, which must be completed in order from left to right, and then addition *or* subtraction, which must be completed in order from left to right. Multiplication and division are on the same level, and addition and subtraction are on the same level; thus, for example, if a division symbol is to the left of a multiplication symbol, divide first.

ACTIVITY: EVALUATING EXPRESSIONS

Students will receive two expressions written on the same piece of paper. One expression has grouping symbols and the other requires grouping symbols. Working individually, students will evaluate the expression that has grouping symbols. They will then find another student who has the same answer. Now working in pairs, students will insert the required grouping symbols in their second expressions.

MATERIALS

One copy of each of the reproducibles, "Expressions for Evaluation, I," "Expressions for Evaluation, II," and "Expressions for Evaluation, III"; scissors or paper cutter for the teacher.

PREPARATION

Make one copy of each reproducible. Cut out the 30 rows of expressions, 1, 2, 3, 4, and so on, contained on the reproducibles. Do not separate the expressions in each row.

PROCEDURE

1. Explain to your students that the order of operations is a set of rules used for evaluating expressions. Review the order of operations and provide a few examples, such as the following:

- $5 \times (2 + 3) - 9$; answer: 16
- $18 \div 2 - (2 + 1)$; answer: 6
- $13 - (5 \times 2 - 1) + 6$; answer: 10

2. Hand out the expressions to your students and explain the activity. Each student will receive one slip of paper containing two expressions. The first expression has grouping symbols in the form of parentheses. The second expression does not. Students will work individually to simplify the first expression. Remind them to use the order of operations. (*Note:* If your class has an even number of students, but fewer than 30, you may eliminate some sets of expressions. In this case, be sure to eliminate pairs of expressions that are equal, for example, number 15 and number 17, both of which have answers of 19. If you have an odd number of students in class, you may ask a volunteer to work with two sets of cards. This student would then work in a group of three rather than a pair when inserting grouping symbols in the second expression.)

3. Explain that after all students have an answer for their first expression, they will find another student in class who has the same answer. Students are to then work together on their second expressions. They must insert grouping symbols so that the second expression equals the value of the first expression. For example, if a first expression equaled 5, they must insert grouping symbols so that the second expression of that set equals 5.

CLOSURE

Discuss the order of operations and strategies that students used to insert grouping symbols. Have students write a reflection to the following question: What would happen if there was no order of operations? Discuss their ideas.

ANSWERS

Expression pairs and their answers follow. 1 and 19 = 23; 2 and 25 = 0; 3 and 26 = 4; 4 and 23 = 17; 5 and 16 = 3; 6 and 27 = 13; 7 and 21 = 15; 8 and 20 = 28; 9 and 29 = 52; 10 and 18 = 10; 11 and 28 = 1; 12 and 30 = 58; 13 and 24 = 16; 14 and 22 = 14; 15 and 17 = 19 The grouping symbols for the second expressions follow. Note that some answers may vary slightly. **(1)** $2 + (4 + 6) \times 2 + 1$ **(2)** $2 \times (3 + 5) - 16$ **(3)** $5 - (2 + 3) + 2 \times 2$ **(4)** $5 \times (3 + 2) - 2 \times 4$ **(5)** $3 \times 3 - (3 + 4) + 1$ **(6)** $8 \times 10 \div (2 \times 5) + 5$ **(7)** $(2 + 7) \times 2 - 3$ **(8)** $4 \times (2 + 7) \div 9 \times 7$ **(9)** $5 \times (2 + 1) \times 3 + 7$ **(10)** $8 \times 5 - 24 - (4 + 2)$ **(11)** $32 \div 8 - (2 + 1)$ **(12)** $(10 + 5) \times 2 + 28$ **(13)** $(6 + 1) \times 2 + 2$ **(14)** $15 - (8 - 6) + 1$ **(15)** $(2 + 3) \times 3 + 4$ **(16)** $(12 - 4) \times 3 \div 8$ **(17)** $10 \div (2 + 3) + 17$ **(18)** $100 \div (1 + 5 + 4)$ **(19)** $45 \div (3 + 6) \times 4 + 3$ **(20)** $6 \times (2 + 2) + 4$ **(21)** $(5 - 4) \times 3 \times 5$ **(22)** $3 \times 4 \times 2 - (11 - 1)$ **(23)** $(4 + 9) \times 2 - 9$ **(24)** $(3 + 4 + 1) \times 2$ **(25)** $4 + 7 - (5 \times 2 + 1)$ **(26)** $5 \times 2 - (9 - 3)$ **(27)** $10 \times 2 - (1 + 2 \times 3)$ **(28)** $15 - 5 - (8 + 1)$ **(29)** $(3 \times 5 + 6) \times 2 + 10$ **(30)** $22 - (10 - 4) + 7 \times 6$

The expressions below are organized in pairs. For example, the first student should receive the expressions in row 1. The second student should receive the expressions in row 2 and so on.

1.	$3 + (6 - 1) \times 4$	$2 + 4 + 6 \times 2 + 1$
2.	$4 - (2 + 1) \div 3 \times 4$	$2 \times 3 + 5 - 16$
3.	$10 \div 5 \times (6 - 4)$	$5 - 2 + 3 + 2 \times 2$
4.	$40 - (3 \times 6 + 4) - 1$	$5 \times 3 + 2 - 2 \times 4$
5.	$30 - (17 + 10)$	$3 \times 3 - 3 + 4 + 1$
6.	$25 \div 5 \times (4 - 1) - 2$	$8 \times 10 \div 2 \times 5 + 5$
7.	$50 \div (9 + 1) + 10$	$2 + 7 \times 2 - 3$
8.	$(3 + 2) \times 5 + 3$	$4 \times 2 + 7 \div 9 \times 7$
9.	$32 + 20 \div (5 - 3) \times 2$	$5 \times 2 + 1 \times 3 + 7$
10.	$(5 + 13) \div 3 + 2 \times 2$	$8 \times 5 - 24 - 4 + 2$

11.	$8 \times 3 \div (2 \times 2 \times 6)$	$32 \div 8 - 2 + 1$
12.	$7 \times 9 - 15 \div (2 + 1)$	$10 + 5 \times 2 + 28$
13.	$49 \div (5 + 2) + 3 \times 3$	$6 + 1 \times 2 + 2$
14.	$9 \times 9 \div 9 + (6 + 4) \div 2$	$15 - 8 - 6 + 1$
15.	$63 \div (3 \times 3) + 3 \times 4$	$2 + 3 \times 3 + 4$
16.	$21 \div 3 \times 2 - (5 + 6)$	$12 - 4 \times 3 \div 8$
17.	$75 \div (5 \times 3) + 14$	$10 \div 2 + 3 + 17$
18.	$16 \div 4 + (10 - 7) \times 2$	$100 \div 1 + 5 + 4$
19.	$(17 + 3) \times 2 - (5 \times 3 + 2)$	$45 \div 3 + 6 \times 4 + 3$
20.	$17 + (6 - 2) \times 4 - 5$	$6 \times 2 + 2 + 4$

21.	$(2 + 5) \times 3 - (1 + 5)$	$5 - 4 \times 3 \times 5$
22.	$(8 + 6) \div 2 + 4 + 3$	$3 \times 4 \times 2 - 11 - 1$
23.	$5 \times (2 + 1) + 2 \div 1$	$4 + 9 \times 2 - 9$
24.	$13 - (5 + 6) + 14$	$3 + 4 + 1 \times 2$
25.	$25 \div (7 - 2) - (2 + 3)$	$4 + 7 - 5 \times 2 + 1$
26.	$64 \div (8 \div 4) \div 8$	$5 \times 2 - 9 - 3$
27.	$50 \div 2 - (2 \times 9 - 2) + 4$	$10 \times 2 - 1 + 2 \times 3$
28.	$5 \times 2 - (10 - 1)$	$15 - 5 - 8 + 1$
29.	$8 + (6 + 4) \times 5 - (4 + 2)$	$3 \times 5 + 6 \times 2 + 10$
30.	$(6 \times 5 + 5) \times 2 - 4 \times 3$	$22 - 10 - 4 + 7 \times 6$

Operations and Algebraic Thinking: 5.OA.2

"Write and interpret numerical expressions."

2. "Write simple expressions that record calculations with numbers, and interpret numerical expressions without evaluating them."

BACKGROUND

Numerical expressions contain numbers and operation symbols. Verbal expressions contain words and phrases. Any mathematical verbal expression can be written as a numerical expression. For example, the expression "subtract 5 from 7 and then multiply by 2" can be written as $(7 - 5) \times 2$.

 ACTIVITY: THE EXPRESSION GAME

Working in pairs or groups of three, students will play a game in which they write numerical expressions when given mathematical verbal expressions. Players who write an expression correctly receive a point. The winner is the player who receives the most points at the end of the game.

MATERIALS

Scissors; reproducible, "Expression Game Cards," for each pair or group of students.

PROCEDURE

1. Explain that key words may be used to indicate basic mathematical operations:

   - Some examples of words that indicate addition include *add, plus, sum, total,* and *in all*.

   - Some examples of words that indicate subtraction include *subtract, minus, difference,* and *fewer than*.

   - Some examples of words that indicate multiplication include *multiply, product,* and *times*.

   - Some examples of words that indicate division include *divide, quotient,* and *half*.

2. Provide a few examples of how to write numerical expressions based on mathematical verbal expressions, such as the following:

   - 3 times the sum of 5 and 2. Answer: $3 \times (5 + 2)$

   - 2 less than 10, divided by 2. Answer: $(10 - 2) \div 2$

   - The sum of 5 and 7 divided by the sum of 4 and 2. Answer: $(5 + 7) \div (4 + 2)$

3. Hand out copies of the reproducible. Explain that it contains 20 cards and that each card has a verbal expression. Students are to cut out the cards, shuffle them, and place them in a pile face down.

4. Explain the game. Students will take turns flipping a card over. Both (or all three) students are to then write the numerical expression that is equivalent to the verbal expression on the card. Correct expressions are worth one point. If both (or all three) students are correct, they each receive one point. Students with incorrect expressions do not receive any points. To determine who is correct, the students must discuss each expression and agree on the answer. If they cannot, you, serving as the referee, provide the correct answer.

5. Remind students to pay close attention to key words and the order of operations. Then start the game.

6. Students may play until time is called or until all the cards have been used.

CLOSURE

Discuss the answers to each card to make sure that the expressions students wrote were correct. Note instances where correct answers varied. Place a few examples on the board and have students share their answers and explain their reasoning.

ANSWERS

Answers may vary slightly; a correct answer for each card follows. **(1)** $10 \div 2 + 5$
(2) $3 \times 6 - 10$ **(3)** $(5 + 6) \times 3$ **(4)** $(9 - 4) \div 5$ **(5)** $(8 + 9) \times 3$ **(6)** $20 \div 5 - 2$ **(7)** $(21 - 8) \times 2$
(8) $3 \times 2 + 7$ **(9)** $3 \times (17 + 4)$ **(10)** $45 \div (4 + 5)$ **(11)** $5 \times (10 - 2)$ **(12)** $(8 + 10) \div 2$
(13) $(17 - 10) \times 4$ **(14)** $36 \div 6 - 4$ **(15)** $7 \times (4 + 3)$ **(16)** $5 \times (9 + 10)$ **(17)** $(20 - 5) \div (2 + 1)$
(18) $4 \times 2 - 8$ **(19)** $9 \times 2 \div 2$ **(20)** $(5 - 3) \times (6 + 4)$

EXPRESSION GAME CARDS

1. Divide 10 by 2, then add 5.	2. Multiply 3 and 6, then subtract 10.	3. Add 5 and 6, then multiply by 3.	4. Subtract 4 from 9, then divide by 5.
5. Find the sum of 8 and 9, then multiply by 3.	6. Divide 20 by 5, then subtract 2.	7. Subtract 8 from 21, then multiply by 2.	8. Find the product of 3 and 2, then add 7.
9. 3 times the sum of 17 and 4.	10. Divide 45 by the sum of 4 and 5.	11. 5 times the difference of 10 and 2.	12. Add 8 and 10, then divide by 2.
13. Subtract 10 from 17, then multiply by 4.	14. Divide 36 by 6, then subtract 4.	15. 7 times the sum of 4 and 3.	16. 5 times the sum of 9 and 10.
17. Subtract 5 from 20, then divide by the sum of 2 and 1.	18. Find the product of 2 and 4, then subtract 8.	19. Multiply 9 and 2, then divide by 2.	20. Subtract 3 from 5, then multiply by the sum of 6 and 4.

Operations and Algebraic Thinking: 5.OA.3

"Analyze patterns and relationships."

> 3. "Generate two numerical patterns using two given rules. Identify apparent relationships between corresponding terms. Form ordered pairs consisting of corresponding terms from the two patterns, and graph the ordered pairs on a coordinate plane."

BACKGROUND

When writing numerical patterns, students should first think of a rule, such as "start at 0 and add 4." Then they may express the rule with numbers. The numbers generated by this rule are 0, 4, 8, 12, 16, ... Here is another rule: "Start at 0 and add 8." This rule would result in the numbers 0, 8, 16, 24, 32, ...

These terms can be expressed as corresponding terms. They can be written as ordered pairs—(0, 0), (4, 8), (8, 16), (12, 24), (16, 32), and so on—and can be graphed in the coordinate plane. (See Geometry: 5.G.1 for instructions on constructing a coordinate plane.) When students look back to analyze these patterns, they should realize that the second number of each ordered pair in this example is twice the first number. This is because 8, which is twice as much as 4, is added in the second pattern.

 ## ACTIVITY: ANALYZING AND GRAPHING PATTERNS

Working in pairs or groups of three, students will develop two numerical patterns. They will express the rule in words and numbers. They will then graph corresponding terms in the coordinate plane. The other students in class will analyze the patterns to determine the rule and relationship between the corresponding terms.

MATERIALS

One sheet of transparent graph paper; one transparency; transparency marker for each pair or group of students; overhead projector.

PROCEDURE

1. Provide a few examples of patterns for your students. One example is 0, 5, 10, 15, 20, ... Ask students to find the rule, which is to start at 0 and add 5. Provide another pattern for your students, such as 0, 15, 30, 45, 60, ... Again, ask students to find the rule, which is to start at 0 and add 15. Ask your students to find a relationship between these two patterns. One relationship is that the terms in the second pattern are three times the corresponding terms in the first pattern.

2. Model how to graph these ordered pairs in the coordinate plane. (See Geometry: 5.G.1.) Depending on the abilities of your students, you may need to review plotting points. Write ordered pairs formed by corresponding terms for the two patterns above. The ordered pairs are (0, 0), (5, 15), (10, 30), (15, 45), and (20, 60). Graph these ordered pairs.

3. Explain that students will now work with their partner, or partners, and create numerical patterns. On a transparency, students will write two number patterns and ordered pairs formed by the corresponding terms of their patterns. On transparent graph paper, they will graph the ordered pairs. They should not write the rule in words for their pattern.

4. When all pairs or groups have completed their patterns, ordered pairs, and graphs, have each show their work to the class on an overhead projector. The other students in class should express the pattern in words and find a numerical relationship between the two patterns.

CLOSURE

Review any patterns that your students had difficulty with. Ask students to identify any patterns that have more than one rule.

Number and Operations in Base Ten: 5.NBT.1

"Understand the place value system."

1. "Recognize that in a multi-digit number, a digit in one place represents 10 times as much as it represents in the place to its right and $\frac{1}{10}$ of what it represents in the place to its left."

BACKGROUND

Our number system is based on powers of ten. Starting at the decimal point and moving left, the place values are ones, tens, hundreds, thousands, ten-thousands, hundred-thousands, millions, and so on. Moving right from the decimal point, the place values are tenths, hundredths, thousandths, ten-thousandths, hundred-thousandths, millionths, and so on.

ACTIVITY: WHAT'S MY NUMBER?

Working in groups of four or five, students will play a game—"What's My Number?"—in which they will write numbers when given clues about place value. Groups will compete against each other. The group with the highest point total at the end of the game is the winner.

MATERIALS

Scissors; reproducibles, "Game Cards for Numbers, I" and "Game Cards for Numbers, II," for each group of students.

PROCEDURE

1. Review place value with your students. It may be helpful to work as a class and make a place value chart as a visual representation.

2. Hand out copies of the reproducibles to each group. Explain that each reproducible contains five cards with clues, using place value, that will help students to find a particular number. Instruct students to cut out the cards and place them face down. (*Note:* Some cards have more clues than other cards.)

3. Explain the rules of the game. One student in each group turns over a card and reads the clues to the rest of the group. The reader may have to read the clues to the group more than once, or the reader may pass the card to the other group members to read for themselves. The group members, including the reader, work together to determine the number, based on the clues. After the group agrees what the number is, a recorder for the group is to write the number and its card number on a sheet of paper. A second

student then turns over the next card and reads the clues to the group, and the procedure is repeated.

4. Explain that the game continues until time is called, or students finish determining numbers for all of the clues. At the end of the game, groups will receive a point for every correct answer. The group with the highest number of points is the winner.

CLOSURE

Provide the answers and have students tally their scores. Announce the winning group. Ask your students questions such as the following: What strategies did you use to find the numbers? What were some key words that helped you find the correct number? How did you decide which number went in each place? How did you decide where the decimal point went, if there was a decimal point?

ANSWERS

(1) 1,205 (2) 654.3 (3) 1.028 (4) 800.08 (5) 956.36 (6) 9,722.09 (7) 5,247.9 (8) 19,721 (9) 0.025 (10) 2,025.1

Card 1

1. The digit in the hundreds place is 2.
2. The digit in the hundreds place is two times the digit in the thousands place.
3. The digit in the ones place is 5 times the digit in the thousands place.
4. The digit in the tens place is 0.

Card 2

1. The digit in the tenths place is half the digit in the hundreds place.
2. The digit in the tens place is 5.
3. The digit in the ones place is 1 less than the digit in the tens place.
4. The digit in the hundreds place is 2 more than the digit in the ones place.

Card 3

1. The digit in the thousandths place is 4 times the digit in the hundredths place.
2. The digit in the hundredths place is 2 times the digit in the ones place.
3. The digit in the ones place is 1.
4. The digit in the tenths place is holding the place.

Card 4

1. The digit in the hundreds place and the digit in the hundredths place are the same.
2. The digit that has no value is in the ones, tens, and tenths places.
3. The digit in the hundreds place is equal to 2 times 4.

Card 5

1. The digit in the tens place is 5.
2. The digits in the ones and hundredths places are the same. Each of these digits is 1 more than the digit in the tens place.
3. The digit in the tenths place is half the digit in the hundredths place.
4. The digit in the hundreds place is 3 times the digit in the tenths place.

Card 6

1. The digits in the thousands place and hundredths place are the same.
2. The digit in the hundreds place is 7.
3. The digit in the hundredths place is 2 more than the digit in the hundreds place.
4. The digits in the ones and tens places are 2 more than the digit in the tenths place.
5. There are no tenths in this number.

Card 7

1. This number has 5 different digits, with one place to the right of the decimal point.
2. The digit in the largest place is 5; the digit in the smallest place is 9.
3. The digit in the ones place is 2 more than the digit in the thousands place.
4. The digit in the tens place is 2 times the digit in the hundreds place.
5. The hundreds place is 7 less than the tenths place.

Card 8

1. This number has 1 ten thousand.
2. The digit in the ten thousands place is the same as the digit in the ones place.
3. The digit in the tens place is 2 times the digit in the ten thousands place.
4. There are 9 thousands in this number.
5. The digit in the hundreds place is 2 less than the digit in the thousands place.

Card 9

1. This number has no ones and no tenths.
2. The digit in the smallest place value is a 5. This digit stands for 5 thousandths.
3. The digit in the hundredths place is 3 less than the digit to its right.

Card 10

1. There are no hundreds in this number.
2. The digits in the thousands place and tens place are the same.
3. There are 5 ones in this number and 2 tens.
4. The digit in the tenths place is 4 less than the digit in the ones place.

Number and Operations in Base Ten: 5.NBT.2

"Understand the place value system."

2. "Explain patterns in the number of zeros of the product when multiplying a number by powers of 10, and explain patterns in the placement of the decimal point when a decimal is multiplied or divided by a power of 10. Use whole-number exponents to denote powers of 10."

BACKGROUND

Our number system is based on powers of 10, where each place is represented by a power of 10. 10^0, 10^1, 10^2, 10^3, and so on are examples of powers of 10, where 10 is the base and a whole number is the exponent. For example, the value of the ones place is 10^0 or 1, the value of the tens place is 10^1, the value of the hundreds place is 10^2, and the value of the thousands place is 10^3.

Once students know how to multiply and divide a number by powers of ten, they can find patterns in the number of zeros and placement of a decimal point. When multiplying by a number that is a power of 10, students must move the decimal point to the right as many places as the exponent. For example, $3 \times 10^2 = 300$. The decimal point, which is understood to be to the right of 3, is moved two places to the right because the exponent is 2. If the number is written without an exponent, such as 100, the decimal point is moved to the right as many places as there are zeros in the number. For example, $3 \times 100 = 300$. The decimal point is moved two places to the right of 3 because 100 has two zeros. When dividing by powers of 10, students must move the decimal point to the left as many places as the exponent. For example, $400 \div 10^2 = 4$. If the number is written without an exponent, such as 100, students must move the decimal point to the left as many places as there are zeros in the number. For example, $400 \div 100 = 4$.

 ## ACTIVITY: CHARTING PATTERNS IN POWERS OF 10

Working in groups, students will create posters that explain and show patterns in multiplying and dividing powers of 10.

MATERIALS

Scissors; glue sticks; markers; crayons; rulers; poster paper; various colors of construction paper for each group.

1. Review place value with your students and especially note the powers of 10 that each place represents. Also note the number of zeros in each power. For example, $10^2 = 100$ and $10^3 = 1,000$.

2. Explain that students are to create posters that are based on place value and that show patterns in the placement of the decimal point when multiplying or dividing by powers of 10.

3. Suggest that students brainstorm ideas before beginning work on their posters. What important ideas do they want to include on their posters? What is the best design for their posters? What examples might they include to illustrate their ideas?

4. Offer some examples of numbers that students might use to identify patterns in the placement of the decimal point when multiplying or dividing by powers of 10, such as: 4×10, 3.5×10^2, and $0.24 \times 1,000$; and $4 \div 10$, $3.5 \div 10^2$, and $24 \div 1,000$.

5. Encourage your students to be creative, but remind them that they must be mathematically accurate.

CLOSURE

Have each group share their poster with the class. During sharing, review place value and patterns in the placement of the decimal point when multiplying or dividing by powers of 10. Display the posters.

Number and Operations in Base Ten: 5.NBT.3

"Understand the place value system."

---

3. "Read, write, and compare decimals to thousandths.

a. "Read and write decimals to thousandths using base-ten numerals, number names, and expanded form.

b. "Compare two decimals to thousandths based on meanings of the digits in each place, using >, =, and < symbols to record the results of comparisons."

BACKGROUND

Numbers can be expressed in words or numerals. When numbers are expressed in words, they are named according to place value. For example, the number 342 is written as "three hundred forty-two"; 23.5 is written as "twenty-three and five tenths."

Numbers can also be written in expanded form, which is the sum of the values of each digit of the number. In expanded form, the number 7,259.6 is written as $7 \times 1,000 + 2 \times 100 + 5 \times 10 + 9 \times 1 + 6 \times \frac{1}{10}$.

ACTIVITY: CREATING NUMBERS

Students will write numbers from clues in which numbers are written using base-ten numerals, number names, and expanded form. They will then compare the numbers using >, =, and < .

MATERIALS

Scissors; glue sticks; one sheet of construction paper; reproducible, "Number Clues," for each student.

PROCEDURE

1. Review place value, with emphasis on writing and reading numbers. Offer some examples, such as the following:

- 2.6 is read "two and six tenths." Note that when writing decimals the word "and" represents the decimal point.

- 17.41 is read "seventeen and forty-one hundredths."

- 0.078 is read "seventy-eight thousandths."

2. Explain that expanded form is written as the sum of the parts of a number. Provide a few examples, such as the following:

- $3,490 = 3 \times 1,000 + 4 \times 100 + 9 \times 10 + 0 \times 1$
- $24.6 = 2 \times 10 + 4 \times 1 + 6 \times \frac{1}{10}$
- $756.485 = 7 \times 100 + 5 \times 10 + 6 \times 1 + 4 \times \frac{1}{10} + 8 \times \frac{1}{100} + 5 \times \frac{1}{1,000}$

3. Hand out copies of the reproducible. Explain that it contains six rows of clues. Students will use the clues in each row to write a number. Note that the clues are not arranged in order according to place value.

4. Explain that students are to cut out the clues in each row. Caution them to cut out and work with one row at a time so as not to mix up the clues from different rows. They are to arrange the clues in order, according to place value, revealing a number. Students are to glue the clues on their construction paper in the correct order, and then write the number after each clue.

5. Explain that after students have written the number for each row, they are to write statements of comparison, as shown on the bottom of the reproducible.

CLOSURE

Discuss the answers of the clues and the comparisons. Instruct your students to create a row of clues of their own. Have them exchange their clues for the clues of a partner and find the number.

ANSWERS

(1) 3,245 (2) 30.879 (3) 2.718 (4) 4,927.3 (5) 2.034 (6) 2.718
Comparisons: (1) $4,927.3 > 3,245$ (2) $2.034 < 30.879$ (3) $2.718 = 2.718$

1	2×100	Three thousand	5×1	4 tens
2	$8 \times \frac{1}{10}$	Seven hundredths	$3 \times 10 + 0 \times 1$	Nine thousandths
3	$7 \times \frac{1}{10}$	2×1	One hundredth	$8 \times \frac{1}{1,000}$
4	$9 \times 100 + 2 \times 10$	Three tenths	Seven ones	$4 \times 1,000$
5	2×1	Zero tenths	Four thousandths	3×0.01
6	Eight thousandths	$1 \times \frac{1}{100}$	$7 \times \frac{1}{10}$	2×1

After you have found the number for each row, do the following:

1. Compare the largest number with the next largest number using the > symbol.

2. Compare the smallest number with the third largest number using the < symbol.

3. Compare the numbers that have the same value using the = symbol.

Number and Operations in Base Ten: 5.NBT.4

"Understand the place value system."

> 4. "Use place value understanding to round decimals to any place."

BACKGROUND

Rounding numbers is a useful skill, particularly for estimation. Following are rules for rounding:

- Find the digit in the place you must round to.

- If the digit to the right of the digit to be rounded is 5 or more, add 1 to the digit you are rounding. Change any digits to the right of the rounded digit to zero.

- If the digit to the right of the digit to be rounded is less than 5, the number you are rounding stays the same. Change any digits to the right of the rounded digit to zero.

- If 9 is in the place you are rounding, and the digit to its right is 5 or more, add 1 to the 9. Because $9 + 1 = 10$, write 0 in place of the 9 and add 1 to the digit to the left. If the digit to the right of 9 is less than 5, the 9 stays the same. Change all digits to the right of the rounded digit to zeros.

- After rounding a decimal, delete any zeros that are not placeholders. (Be sure that students understand that there must always be a digit, even if it is zero, in the place they are rounding to.)

 ## ACTIVITY: ROUND THE NUMBER

Working in groups, students will play "Round the Number." They will follow the directions on cards that ask them to round decimals to a specific place.

MATERIALS

Scissors; reproducible, "Round the Number Game Cards," for each group of students.

PROCEDURE

1. Review the rules of rounding with your students, as noted in the Background. Provide examples, such as the following:

   - Round 4.732 to the nearest tenth. Answer: 4.7

   - Round 0.958 to the nearest hundredth. Answer: 0.96

   - Round 81.396 to the nearest hundredth. Answer: 81.40

2. Distribute copies of the reproducible. Explain that it contains 20 cards, each with a number to be rounded to a specific place.

3. Explain the game. Students are to cut out the cards and place them face down. Students in a group play against each other. Each will take turns selecting a card. All of the members of a group are to follow the directions on the card and round the number to the place indicated on the card. Students will record and compare their answers to determine who is correct. Each student receives a point for every correct answer. If students disagree and cannot determine who is correct, you will serve as the referee.

4. Explain that the game is over when time is called or students have completed all of the cards. The winner in each group is the player who has the most points at the end of the game.

CLOSURE

Announce the rounded numbers so that students can verify the winners of their groups. Discuss any numbers that students found confusing or difficult to round. On another day, have groups write their own game cards, exchange their cards with another group, and play another game of "Round the Number."

ANSWERS

(1) 2.5 (2) 4 (3) 19.8 (4) 8.03 (5) 25.90 (6) 7 (7) 810 (8) 300 (9) 6,827.16 (10) 15.3 (11) 5.1 (12) 17.83 (13) 1,000 (14) 62.00 (15) 10 (16) 720 (17) 100 (18) 8,910 (19) 341.1 (20) 10,000

1. Round 2.54 to the nearest tenth.	**2.** Round 3.723 to the nearest whole number.	**3.** Round 19.75 to the nearest tenth.	**4.** Round 8.034 to the nearest hundredth.
5. Round 25.895 to the nearest hundredth.	**6.** Round 6.82 to the nearest whole number.	**7.** Round 812.8 to the nearest ten.	**8.** Round 298.09 to the nearest hundred.
9. Round 6,827.158 to the nearest hundredth.	**10.** Round 15.283 to the nearest tenth.	**11.** Round 5.092 to the nearest tenth.	**12.** Round 17.829 to the nearest hundredth.
13. Round 1,492 to the nearest thousand.	**14.** Round 61.995 to the nearest hundredth.	**15.** Round 12.072 to the nearest ten.	**16.** Round 719.954 to the nearest whole number.
17. Round 99.926 to the nearest hundred.	**18.** Round 8,914.94 to the nearest ten.	**19.** Round 341.05 to the nearest tenth.	**20.** Round 9,999.999 to the nearest thousand.

Number and Operations in Base Ten: 5.NBT.5

"Perform operations with multi-digit whole numbers and with decimals to hundredths."

5. "Fluently multiply multi-digit whole numbers using the standard algorithm."

BACKGROUND

In mathematics, an algorithm is a procedure or method for solving a problem. Understanding the standard multiplication algorithm is essential for students to multiply fluently. Following are the steps for multiplying 76×35:

$$
\begin{array}{r}
35 \\
\times 76 \\
\hline
210 \\
+ 2450 \\
\hline
2{,}660
\end{array}
$$

210 Multiply by the ones digit first. $6 \times 35 = 210$
+ 2450 Multiply by the tens digit. $70 \times 35 = 2450$
2,660 Add the partial products. $210 + 2450 = 2{,}660$

For larger numbers, the same process is followed for each place value in the multiplier before all the partial products are summed.

ACTIVITY 1: MODELING MULTIPLICATION

Students will go to a Web site where they will create multiplication problems using the standard algorithm. The computer will help them to model these problems.

MATERIALS

Computers with Internet access for students; computer with Internet access and digital projector for the teacher.

PROCEDURE

1. Instruct your students to go to http://nlvm.usu.edu/. They should click in the grades "3–5" column on the "Numbers and Operations" row and then scroll down to and click on "Rectangle Multiplication." They will see a grid that models multiplication.

2. Demonstrate how to use this Web site. Click on "Common" on the bottom of the screen. A problem will appear, and the computer will model the standard algorithm for multiplication on a grid.

3. Do a few examples as a class. Explain that the numbers in the problem are shown in different colors on the grid. Moving the buttons on the side and on the bottom of the grid changes the problem. With each change the computer models the problem for students and provides the steps for multiplication using the standard algorithm. Make sure students are comfortable with the procedure before allowing them to work independently.

4. Allow your students time to explore multiplication on the Web site by creating at least three problems of their own.

5. Next, instruct them to find the products of three problems that you provide. Because of the limitation of the Web site, the factors must be 30 or less. Students are to solve the problems using the standard algorithm, and then check their product on the Web site.

CLOSURE

Have students write an exit ticket explaining the standard algorithm for multiplication.

ACTIVITY 2: FINDING ERRORS IN MULTIPLICATION

Students will find and correct errors on a fictitious quiz that focuses on multiplying multi-digit whole numbers.

MATERIALS

Reproducible, "Multi-Digit Multiplication Quiz," for each student.

PROCEDURE

1. Review the standard algorithm for multiplication with your students. If necessary, provide a few example problems.

2. Hand out copies of the reproducible. Explain that this is a quiz taken by a fictional student named John. He has made several mistakes on his quiz, and it is the task of your students to find his errors and correct his answers. Some answers are correct.

3. Allow students time to find and correct all the errors.

CLOSURE

Have students check their answers with a partner. Discuss the mistakes they found. Did they find the same mistakes? Did they find all the mistakes? How could they be certain? Did they search for errors in the problems in different ways? If yes, what were the different ways?

Name: John

Corrected by: _____

MULTI-DIGIT MULTIPLICATION QUIZ

1. $\begin{array}{r} 21 \\ \times\,42 \\ \hline 42 \\ +\,84 \\ \hline 126 \end{array}$	2. $\begin{array}{r} 24 \\ \times\,36 \\ \hline 144 \\ +\,720 \\ \hline 884 \end{array}$	3. $\begin{array}{r} 38 \\ \times\,75 \\ \hline 190 \\ +\,2660 \\ \hline 2{,}850 \end{array}$
4. $\begin{array}{r} 40 \\ \times\,56 \\ \hline 24 \\ +\,2000 \\ \hline 2{,}024 \end{array}$	5. $\begin{array}{r} 43 \\ \times\,59 \\ \hline 387 \\ +\,2150 \\ \hline 2{,}537 \end{array}$	6. $\begin{array}{r} 700 \\ \times\,96 \\ \hline 4200 \\ +\,63000 \\ \hline 67{,}200 \end{array}$
7. $\begin{array}{r} 308 \\ \times\,45 \\ \hline 1540 \\ +\,12320 \\ \hline 13{,}860 \end{array}$	8. $\begin{array}{r} 175 \\ \times\,82 \\ \hline 340 \\ +\,14000 \\ \hline 14{,}340 \end{array}$	9. $\begin{array}{r} 387 \\ \times\,26 \\ \hline 2322 \\ +\,7690 \\ \hline 10{,}012 \end{array}$

Number and Operations in Base Ten: 5.NBT.6

"Perform operations with multi-digit whole numbers and with decimals to hundredths."

> 6. "Find whole-number quotients of whole numbers with up to four-digit dividends and two-digit divisors, using strategies based on place value, the properties of operations, and/or the relationship between multiplication and division. Illustrate and explain calculation by using equations, rectangular arrays, and/or area models."

BACKGROUND

In a division problem, the number that is being divided is called the dividend; the number that divides the dividend is called the divisor; and the answer is called the quotient. There are several ways to solve division problems, including:

- Using long division
- Finding a connection between multiplication and division
- Using rectangular arrays
- Using area models

ACTIVITY 1: PIECING TOGETHER DIVISION

Students will build division problems from given lists of numbers.

MATERIALS

Reproducible, "Finding Dividends, Divisors, and Quotients," for each student.

PROCEDURE

1. Review the process of division and provide some examples.

2. Distribute copies of the reproducible. Explain that it has eight rows with four numbers in each row.

3. Instruct your students to work with the numbers in each row. Of the numbers in the row, they are to find three that can form a division problem, identifying the dividend, divisor, and quotient. Explain that there will be no remainders. Also note that one number in the row will not be used. You might also want to mention that because divisors and quotients can be switched, two problems may be found for each row.

ACTIVITY 2: MODELING DIVISION

Students will use virtual manipulatives and rectangular arrays on a Web site to model division.

MATERIALS

Computers with Internet access for students; computer with Internet access and digital projector for the teacher.

PROCEDURE

1. Instruct your students to go to http://nlvm.usu.edu/. They should click in the grades "3–5" column on the "Numbers and Operations" row and then scroll down to and click on "Rectangle Division." They will see a division array and information on the right side of the screen explaining a division problem.

2. Demonstrate how this Web site works. Start by working with the 10-by-10 grid and click on "Show Me." Explain that students can change the divisor to model a division problem by moving the button on the left up or down. They can change the dividend on the lower right by clicking on either the up button or the down button. Note that the array adjusts to model the problem. Information is provided on the right side of the screen.

3. Choose a problem to discuss as a class, such as $35 \div 5$. Students should already know that the quotient is 7. Explain that the rectangular array shows that there are 7 groups of 5 in 35, with nothing left over. This division problem is linked to multiplication by showing that $5 \times 7 = 35$.

4. Instruct your students to create another problem, such as $35 \div 9$, which is asking how many groups of 9 are in 35. Tell your students to move the button on the left side of the screen to 9 and make sure that the dividend is 35. This creates a 9 by 3 rectangular array. Explain that this array represents 3 groups of 9 within 35. Note that there are also

8 squares shaded in a different color. These 8 squares represent the remainder. Relate this division problem to its multiplication problem: $3 \times 9 + 8 = 35$.

5. Explain to your students that they are to complete at least 10 problems. They should click on "Test Me" on the bottom of the screen and the computer will generate a new problem. (*Note:* Depending on the problem, the array and grid will automatically change. Clicking on a different grid will change the problem.) Students are to change the dimensions of the array by changing the divisor according to the problem. Then they should consider the array, and complete the problem on the right by filling in the empty boxes. When they click on "Check," the computer will check their answer. They can move on to another problem by clicking on "New Problem." As students work, they should record their problems and answers for the discussion during Closure.

CLOSURE

Discuss the activity. Ask students what problems they found to be difficult. Have a few students share their hardest problems.

1.	24	28	56	1,344
2.	45	44	2,070	46
3.	47	37	81	2,997
4.	216	3	72	13
5.	53	2,436	58	42
6.	528	6	88	83
7.	56	448	8	6
8.	18	476	28	17

Number and Operations in Base Ten: 5.NBT.7

"Perform operations with multi-digit whole numbers and with decimals to hundredths."

> 7. "Add, subtract, multiply, and divide decimals to hundredths, using concrete models or drawings and strategies based on place value, properties of operations, and/or the relationship between addition and subtraction; relate the strategy to a written method and explain the reasoning used."

BACKGROUND

The procedures for adding, subtracting, multiplying, and dividing decimals are similar to the procedures for performing the basic operations with whole numbers, with the exception of placement of the decimal point. To master these operations, an understanding of place value is essential.

 ACTIVITY 1: PLACE VALUE, ADDITION, AND SUBTRACTION OF DECIMALS

Working in pairs or groups of three, students will write addition and subtraction problems involving decimals, based on specific instructions and place values.

MATERIALS

Scissors; glue sticks; unlined paper; reproducibles, "Build a Problem" and "Number Cards," for each pair or group of students.

PROCEDURE

1. If necessary, review the procedures for adding and subtracting decimals. Also, your students might find a review of place value helpful.

2. Hand out copies of the reproducibles. Explain that "Build a Problem" contains instructions for building six problems: three decimal addition problems and three decimal subtraction problems. The instructions are based on place value. Cards containing numbers are on the reproducible, "Number Cards." These cards contain the numbers students will use to create the problems, as well as the answers to the problems. Note that each problem requires three cards: two cards for the problem and one card for the answer.

3. Explain that students are to cut out the cards. After cutting out the cards, they should match the cards to create problems and answers that satisfy the instructions. Caution them to start with the first problem and work in order. After they have created a problem,

they should place the numbers that make up the problem, including its answer, on their unlined paper. They should include +, −, and = signs as necessary. After they have "built" all of the problems, they should glue the numbers and answers that make up each problem on their paper. (Gluing after they have built all of the problems allows them to adjust numbers if they make a mistake.) Note that some cards will not be used.

CLOSURE

Check students' problems and answers. Instruct them to write an explanation of the strategies they used to build their problems.

ANSWERS

(1) 5.82 + 7.45 = 13.27 **(2)** 16.93 − 14.03 = 2.9 **(3)** 0.06 + 7.25 = 7.31
(4) 9.06 − 3.4 = 5.66 **(5)** 1.7 + 11.91 = 13.61 **(6)** 20.94 − 17.35 = 3.59

ACTIVITY 2: MODELING MULTIPLICATION AND DIVISION OF DECIMALS

Students will model multiplication and division of decimals on graph paper. They will relate the models to the standard algorithms.

MATERIALS

Ruler; colored pencils; crayons; graph paper for each student.

PROCEDURE

1. Explain that students will model multiplication and division of decimals.

2. Instruct them to mark off a 10-by-10 square on graph paper.

3. Together as a class, work on the following two examples.

   - First model 0.3 × 0.2. Instruct your students to use a colored pencil, or crayon, to lightly color 2 tenths vertically within the 10-by-10 square. Note that 2 tenths (2 columns) is equivalent to 20 hundredths (20 graph-paper squares). Students should then use a different color to color 3 tenths on the grid horizontally. Note that 3 tenths (3 rows) is equivalent to 30 hundredths and that the two colors will overlap on 6 squares on the grid. Ask your students what the product is based on their model. They should realize that the product is represented by the region that is colored with both colors. Six squares are shaded with both colors; therefore, the product is 6 hundredths.

- Instruct your students to mark off another 10-by-10 square on graph paper. Now model a division problem: 0.56 ÷ 0.07. Students should use a colored pencil, or crayon, to lightly color 56 hundredths vertically on the grid. Next they should use a different color to shade 7 of the 56 squares that they already shaded. After they have shaded 7 hundredths, ask them to shade the remaining 49 hundredths in groups of 7. They may choose to use a different color for each group, or to outline each group more darkly. Ask them to use the model to identify the quotient. The quotient is 8 because there are 8 groups of 7 hundredths in 56 hundredths.

4. Present these problems to your students: (1) 0.8×0.9; (2) $0.48 \div 0.04$; (3) 0.6×0.5; (4) $0.28 \div 0.07$. Instruct your students to complete models for these problems on graph paper, showing the solutions. If time permits, add more problems.

CLOSURE

Discuss the answers. Ask questions such as the following: How were the models similar? How were they different? How can you use each type of model to find the corresponding multiplication or division problem? Have students write a reflection on the connection between multiplication and division of decimals.

ANSWERS

(1) 0.72; 72 squares are in the overlapping regions. (2) 12; 12 groups of 4 hundredths are formed. (3) 0.30; 30 squares are in the overlapping regions. (4) 4; 4 groups of 7 hundredths are formed.

BUILD A PROBLEM

Directions: Follow the clues to create decimal addition and subtraction problems and their answers. Start with problem 1 and work in order. Use the Number Cards to create the problems and answers. Each card will be used only once. Two cards will not be used.

1. The problem's first addend has 5 ones. The other addend has 4 tenths. The sum has 7 hundredths.

2. The problem starts with a number that has 3 hundredths. The number that is subtracted has 3 hundredths. The answer has 2 ones.

3. The problem's first addend has 0 tenths. The other addend has 2 tenths. The sum has 1 hundredth.

4. The number that starts the problem has 6 hundredths. The number that is subtracted has 4 tenths. The answer has 5 ones.

5. The problem's first addend has 7 tenths. The other addend has 1 ten. The sum has 1 ten and 3 ones.

6. The number that starts the problem has 0 ones. The number that is subtracted has 5 hundredths. The answer has 5 tenths.

NUMBER CARDS

7.31	9.06	5.82	16.93	3.59
3.4	11.91	1.7	1.45	13.61
2.9	7.25	14.03	6.98	7.45
5.66	20.94	13.27	0.06	17.35

Number and Operations—Fractions: 5.NF.1

"Use equivalent fractions as a strategy to add and subtract fractions."

> 1. "Add and subtract fractions with unlike denominators (including mixed numbers) by replacing given fractions with equivalent fractions in such a way as to produce an equivalent sum or difference of fractions with like denominators."

BACKGROUND

To add or subtract fractions, the denominators must be the same. If the denominators are different, students must write equivalent fractions that have the same denominator. For example, to add $\frac{1}{4}$ and $\frac{2}{3}$, students must find a common denominator. To find the least common denominator, students should find the least common multiple of 4 and 3, which is 12. They must then change each fraction to an equivalent fraction with a denominator of 12. $\frac{1}{4} \times \frac{3}{3} = \frac{3}{12}$ and $\frac{2}{3} \times \frac{4}{4} = \frac{8}{12}$ The problem is rewritten as $\frac{3}{12} + \frac{8}{12} = \frac{11}{12}$.

 ACTIVITY 1: ADDING PARTS OF A WHOLE

Students will work at a Web site where they will add and model fractions with unlike denominators.

MATERIALS

Computers with Internet access for students; computer with Internet access and digital projector for the teacher.

PROCEDURE

1. Review an example of adding fractions with unlike denominators, such as the example provided in the Background.

2. Instruct students to go to http://nlvm.usu.edu/. They should click in the grades "3–5" column on the "Numbers and Operations" row and then scroll down to and click on "Fractions—Adding." They will see fractions that they must rename so that the denominators are the same. They will also see models that visually represent the fractions. Tell your students which degree of difficulty they should check: Easier, Harder, or Hardest.

3. Demonstrate how to use the Web site. Ask students to write the equivalent fractions that are presented. To help them write the equivalent fractions, they may use the models and change the denominators by clicking on the up or down arrows. The numbers below the

models indicate the denominator of the fraction while the shaded parts of the model indicate the numerator. Students should then write an equivalent fraction, or fractions, by writing numbers in the blank spaces. After writing equivalent fractions, they should click on "Check." If they are correct, an addition problem will appear. To help them solve the problem, students may drag the colored portions of the models to the right. Or they may simply solve the problem and click "Check." If they are correct, the model will adjust to reflect the answer. They should then click on "New Problem."

4. Instruct your students to continue working on the Web site and complete at least five problems. They are to record their problems on paper so that they can discuss the problems during Closure.

CLOSURE

Select a few students to write one of their problems on the board and explain the process for finding common denominators and writing equivalent fractions.

ACTIVITY 2: FINDING A MATCH

Working in teams of two or three, students will play a game called "Finding a Match." Two teams will play against each other. Opposing teams will be given one set of 10 cards that contain addition and subtraction of fraction problems with a missing number. Each team will also receive an identical set of cards that contain equivalent fractions that can be used to complete the problems. The winner is the team with more points at the end of the game.

MATERIALS

Scissors; reproducibles, "Finding a Match Problem Cards" and "Equivalent Fraction Cards," for each team.

PROCEDURE

1. Review adding and subtracting fractions, noting that the fractions must have like denominators. Provide a few examples, such as $\frac{3}{4} + \frac{1}{8} = \frac{6}{8} + \frac{1}{8} = \frac{7}{8}$. Be sure students know how to write equivalent fractions.

2. Distribute copies of the reproducibles. Explain that "Finding a Match Problem Cards" contains 10 cards with addition and subtraction problems with a missing fraction or mixed number. Students should cut out the cards and place them face down between the two teams. "Equivalent Fraction Cards" contains two sets of cards that have fractions or mixed numbers. Students are to cut out these cards as well, keeping a set of fraction cards for each team. Note that the game requires only one set of problem cards, but each team needs its own set of the equivalent fraction cards.

3. Explain the game. Two teams play against each other. The problem cards are to be placed face down between the teams. One set of equivalent fraction cards should be set in front of each team. The first team will flip a problem card over. Both teams then try to find the fraction or mixed number card that completes the problem correctly. Emphasize that students must recognize equivalent fractions to complete the problems. Students should simplify as necessary. After completing the first problem, the process continues with the second team flipping a problem card over. Upon completion of the game, teams will receive one point for each problem they solve correctly. Note that not all of the fraction cards will be used.

4. Have your students record each problem so that you may discuss the answers and tally the scores when the game is over. The games end when all of the teams have completed all of the problems.

CLOSURE

Provide the answers to the problems, have students add their scores, and announce the winners of the games. Discuss the steps for finding equivalent fractions and common denominators. You may want to have your students develop their own cards for this game. They can then play the game as a review at a later date.

ANSWERS

(1) $\frac{1}{3}$ (2) $\frac{8}{11}$ (3) $\frac{2}{7}$ (4) $\frac{7}{12}$ (5) $2\frac{1}{3}$ (6) $\frac{9}{10}$ (7) $\frac{1}{4}$ (8) $\frac{1}{8}$ (9) $\frac{1}{5}$ (10) $2\frac{1}{4}$

1. $\frac{5}{9} + \frac{?}{?} = \frac{8}{9}$	2. $\frac{?}{?} - \frac{2}{3} = \frac{2}{33}$
3. $1\frac{?}{?} + 2\frac{1}{2} = 3\frac{11}{14}$	4. $\frac{?}{?} - \frac{1}{3} = \frac{1}{4}$
5. $4\frac{3}{4} - ?\frac{?}{?} = 2\frac{5}{12}$	6. $\frac{?}{?} - \frac{1}{2} = \frac{2}{5}$
7. $\frac{1}{20} + \frac{?}{?} = \frac{3}{10}$	8. $\frac{?}{?} + \frac{3}{24} = \frac{1}{4}$
9. $1\frac{1}{4} + 2\frac{?}{?} = 3\frac{9}{20}$	10. $4\frac{7}{10} - ?\frac{?}{?} = 2\frac{9}{20}$

EQUIVALENT FRACTION CARDS (2 SETS PER GAME)

$\dfrac{1}{5}$	$\dfrac{1}{3}$	$\dfrac{7}{12}$	$\dfrac{2}{7}$
$\dfrac{1}{4}$	$\dfrac{5}{6}$	$\dfrac{1}{8}$	$3\dfrac{1}{2}$
$2\dfrac{1}{4}$	$\dfrac{8}{11}$	$2\dfrac{1}{3}$	$\dfrac{9}{10}$

$\dfrac{1}{5}$	$\dfrac{1}{3}$	$\dfrac{7}{12}$	$\dfrac{2}{7}$
$\dfrac{1}{4}$	$\dfrac{5}{6}$	$\dfrac{1}{8}$	$3\dfrac{1}{2}$
$2\dfrac{1}{4}$	$\dfrac{8}{11}$	$2\dfrac{1}{3}$	$\dfrac{9}{10}$

Number and Operations—Fractions: 5.NF.2

"Use equivalent fractions as a strategy to add and subtract fractions."

2. "Solve word problems involving addition and subtraction of fractions referring to the same whole, including cases of unlike denominators, e.g., by using visual fraction models or equations to represent the problem. Use benchmark fractions and number sense of fractions to estimate mentally and assess the reasonableness of answers."

BACKGROUND

Writing equations and drawing models are useful strategies for solving addition and subtraction of fraction problems. No matter what strategy, or strategies, students use to solve problems, they should always ask themselves if their answers make sense.

ACTIVITY: ADDING AND SUBTRACTING FRACTIONS

Working in pairs or groups of three, students will solve word problems by adding and subtracting fractions. They will write equations and draw models that represent the problems.

MATERIALS

Rulers; compasses; unlined paper; reproducible, "Estimating, Adding, and Subtracting Fractions," for each pair or group of students.

PROCEDURE

1. Explain that equations and models are useful for representing fraction problems and can be helpful for finding solutions. For example, a half of a pie can be represented by $\frac{1}{2} \times 1 = \frac{1}{2}$ or a circle divided into 2 equal parts with 1 part being shaded. Ask your students for examples of other situations that can be represented by equations and modeled by fractions.

2. Distribute copies of the reproducible. Explain that it contains four word problems. Students are to answer the questions and solve the problems. For each problem they must also write an equation and draw a model. They should draw their models, write equations, and provide the answers to the problems on the unlined paper. Encourage students to use their rulers and/or compasses to draw accurate models.

Discuss the answers to the problems on the reproducible. Ask students how accurate their estimates were, and how they determined their estimates. Have students share their equations and models with other groups. Select some problems and challenge students to find another model that supports their answer.

ANSWERS

Estimates and models will vary; models should support student's answers. **(1)** $\frac{1}{4} = \frac{2}{8}$; $\frac{2}{8} + \frac{1}{8} = \frac{3}{8}$ **(2)** $\frac{1}{3} = \frac{2}{6}$ and $\frac{1}{2} = \frac{3}{6}$; $\frac{3}{6} - \frac{2}{6} = \frac{1}{6}$ cup **(3)** $\frac{2}{3} = \frac{4}{6}$ and $\frac{1}{2} = \frac{3}{6}$; $\frac{4}{6} + \frac{3}{6} = \frac{7}{6} = 1\frac{1}{6}$ inches **(4)** $\frac{3}{4} = \frac{9}{12}$ and $\frac{2}{3} = \frac{8}{12}$; $\frac{9}{12} - \frac{8}{12} = \frac{1}{12}$ Annie completed $\frac{1}{12}$ more of the levels.

Directions: Answer the questions and solve the problems.

1. Carmella's mom baked Carmella and her younger brother Anthony a homemade pizza. Carmella ate $\frac{1}{4}$ of the pizza and Anthony ate $\frac{1}{8}$. Estimate about how much of the pizza the two children ate. Write an equation and draw a model to represent the problem. Now solve the problem to find how much of the pizza the two children ate. Was your estimate accurate?

2. Leah's cookie recipe calls for $\frac{1}{3}$ cup of small candies. She has $\frac{1}{2}$ cup of candies from the last time she baked. Estimate about how much candy she will have left over. Write an equation and draw a model to represent the problem. Now solve the problem to find how much candy will be left over. Was your estimate accurate?

3. A recent storm dropped $\frac{2}{3}$ inch of rain on Brian's town. During another storm, $\frac{1}{2}$ inch of rain fell. Estimate about how much rain fell on Brian's town during these two storms. Write an equation and draw a model to represent the problem. Now solve the problem to find how much rain fell during the two storms. Was your estimate accurate?

4. Annie and Raul were playing a computer game. A player has to complete many levels to win. Annie completed $\frac{3}{4}$ of the levels needed to win and Raul completed $\frac{2}{3}$. Estimate who completed more levels. Write an equation and draw a model to represent the problem. Now solve the problem to find the difference between how much of the levels the two children completed. Was your estimate accurate?

Number and Operations—Fractions: 5.NF.3

"Apply and extend previous understandings of multiplication and division to multiply and divide fractions."

3. "Interpret a fraction as division of the numerator by the denominator $\left(\frac{a}{b} = a \div b\right)$. Solve word problems involving division of whole numbers leading to answers in the form of fractions or mixed numbers, e.g., by using visual fraction models or equations to represent the problem."

BACKGROUND

A fraction represents division of the numerator by the denominator. The fraction bar can be thought of as a division sign. For example, $\frac{1}{2}$ can be thought of as $1 \div 2$.

 ACTIVITY: RELATING FRACTIONS TO DIVISION

Working first individually, then in groups, students will brainstorm to generate a list of at least three examples of real-life situations that show fractions as the division of a numerator by a denominator. Based on the situations, they will create problems, draw models, and write equations that will be used to solve the problems.

MATERIALS

Ruler; compass; unlined paper for each student.

PROCEDURE

1. Present the following problem: Sam, Tyler, Sophie, and Jorge buy two large pizzas. If they share the pizzas equally, what fraction of a whole pizza does each person eat? Draw a model and write an equation to help you solve the problem.

2. Provide a few minutes for your students to work on this problem individually. Then have them share their answers, equations, and models with a partner.

3. Have volunteers show their work on the board and explain how they solved the problem.

4. Explain that this problem could be modeled by the equation 2 ÷ 4 because four friends are sharing two pizzas equally. A possible model is shown below. The two circles, representing the pizzas, are split into 4 equal pieces each, showing that four people are splitting the pizza. Each person would receive $\frac{2}{4}$ or $\frac{1}{2}$ of a pizza.

 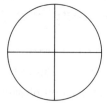

5. Explain that students will now work in their groups and create similar problems. First, they are to brainstorm a list of at least three real-life situations that show fractions as division of a numerator by a denominator. Suggest that they consider the example of the shared pizzas and generate some situations of their own, such as boxes of markers shared by four students or dividing a small birthday cake among six partygoers.

6. After groups create their lists, ask each group to share its list. Make sure that the situations they developed are applicable to division.

7. Instruct the groups to write three word problems, based on their lists.

8. After each group has completed writing their word problems, instruct them to provide solutions using models and writing equations on a separate sheet of paper.

9. Have each group trade their problems with another group. (They should not trade models and equations at this time.) Groups are to solve each other's problems, creating their own models and writing equations. When each group has solved the other's problems, have them trade the original models and equations to double-check their work.

CLOSURE

Discuss students' work. Have volunteers share a problem and show their model and equation on the board. Ask students: How can models and equations help in finding the solution to a problem?

Number and Operations—Fractions: 5.NF.4

"Apply and extend previous understandings of multiplication and division to multiply and divide fractions."

4. "Apply and extend previous understandings of multiplication to multiply a fraction or whole number by a fraction.

   a. "Interpret the product $\left(\frac{a}{b}\right) \times q$ as a parts of a partition of q into b equal parts; equivalently, as the result of a sequence of operations $a \times q \div b$.

   b. "Find the area of a rectangle with fractional side lengths by tiling it with unit squares of the appropriate unit fraction side lengths, and show that the area is the same as would be found by multiplying the side lengths. Multiply fractional side lengths to find areas of rectangles, and represent fraction products as rectangular areas."

BACKGROUND

The standard algorithm for multiplying a fraction by a fraction is to find the product of the numerators and find the product of the denominators, and then write the product of the numerators over the product of the denominators. Simplify, if necessary. For example, $\frac{1}{2} \times \frac{2}{3} = \frac{2}{6} = \frac{1}{3}$.

   In the case of multiplying a whole number by a fraction, the whole number must first be written as an improper fraction. The process for multiplying a fraction by a fraction is then followed. For example, $\frac{1}{3} \times 2 = \frac{1}{3} \times \frac{2}{1} = \frac{2}{3}$.

   Students can model multiplication of fractions using rectangles. In the problem $\frac{1}{2} \times \frac{2}{3}$, for example, students may begin by drawing 1 whole as shown below in Step 1. They would then divide the whole into 3 equal parts and shade 2 of these parts as shown in Step 2. Multiplying by $\frac{1}{2}$ divides the whole into 2 equal parts as shown in Step 3. Since the numerator is 1, note that 1 of the 2 equal parts is shaded in Step 4 (the top three squares). The region that is shaded twice shows the product, which is $\frac{2}{6}$ or $\frac{1}{3}$.

Step 1   Step 2   Step 3   Step 4

ACTIVITY 1: MODELING MULTIPLICATION OF FRACTIONS

Working in pairs or groups of three, students will receive a model of a multiplication problem. They are to write an equation, based on the model, and then write a story context for the problem.

MATERIALS

One copy of reproducible, "Modeling Multiplication of Fractions."

PREPARATION

After making a copy of the reproducible, cut out the 10 models, one for each pair or group of students. (*Note:* For large classes, more than one pair or group may work with the same model, in which case you will need two copies of the reproducible.)

PROCEDURE

1. Explain the model for the problem $\frac{1}{2} \times \frac{2}{3}$ to your students as shown in the Background. Suggest that students copy it so that they may refer to it later, if necessary.

2. Hand out a model of a multiplication problem to each pair or group of students. Explain that the model is similar to the example you just discussed.

3. Explain that students are to write an equation that represents their model. They are then to write a story context for the problem. They should then solve the problem.

CLOSURE

Discuss the models, equations, and answers. Have each pair or group of students share their work and their story context with another pair or group. Instruct students to discuss if the story context matches the problem, and if the equation is an accurate representation of the model.

ANSWERS

Story contexts will vary, but should represent the problem. Following are the equations that correspond to each model. **(1)** $\frac{1}{2} \times \frac{3}{5} = \frac{3}{10}$ **(2)** $\frac{1}{2} \times \frac{1}{2} = \frac{1}{4}$ **(3)** $\frac{1}{3} \times \frac{2}{5} = \frac{2}{15}$ **(4)** $\frac{1}{2} \times \frac{5}{6} = \frac{5}{12}$
(5) $\frac{1}{3} \times \frac{2}{3} = \frac{2}{9}$ **(6)** $\frac{3}{4} \times \frac{3}{5} = \frac{9}{20}$ **(7)** $\frac{1}{2} \times \frac{1}{3} = \frac{1}{6}$ **(8)** $\frac{1}{2} \times \frac{5}{7} = \frac{5}{14}$ **(9)** $\frac{3}{5} \times \frac{4}{5} = \frac{12}{25}$ **(10)** $\frac{1}{2} \times \frac{7}{9} = \frac{7}{18}$

ACTIVITY 2: TILING RECTANGLES WITH FRACTIONS

Working in pairs or groups of three, students will find the areas of rectangles by tiling. They will then check their answers by multiplying the lengths of the sides.

MATERIALS

Scissors; glue sticks; one large sheet of construction paper (in a color other than white, to provide a contrast with the unit squares used for tiling); reproducible, "Unit Squares for Constructing Rectangles," for each pair or group of students.

PROCEDURE

1. Explain that the area of a rectangle can be found by multiplying length times width, $A = l \times w$. This same method can be used whether the dimensions of the rectangle are whole numbers or fractions. Provide the following example:

   A rectangle is 2 units long by $\frac{1}{2}$ unit wide: $A = l \times w = 2 \times \frac{1}{2} = \frac{2}{2} = 1$ square unit.

2. Explain that the area of a rectangle can also be found by tiling the rectangle with squares of the appropriate side length. Present the previous example of the rectangle that is 2 units long by $\frac{1}{2}$ unit wide.

   - Draw the rectangle.

   2 units / $\frac{1}{2}$ unit

   - Tile the rectangle with squares that are $\frac{1}{2}$ unit by $\frac{1}{2}$ unit.

   2 units / $\frac{1}{2}$ unit

   - Ask your students to find the area of each square that is $\frac{1}{2}$ unit long by $\frac{1}{2}$ unit wide. Students should realize that the area is $\frac{1}{4}$ square unit because $\frac{1}{2} \times \frac{1}{2} = \frac{1}{4}$. Ask your students to find the area of the rectangle by using the squares. Students should then realize that the area of the rectangle is 1 square unit, because the rectangle is covered with 4 squares and the area of each square is $\frac{1}{4}$ square unit ($4 \times \frac{1}{4} = 1$).

   - Instruct your students to find the area of the rectangle by using the formula. They should find that the area is 1 square unit because $2 \times \frac{1}{2} = \frac{2}{2} = 1$. Note that the area they found by tiling is the same as the area they found by using the formula.

3. Hand out copies of the reproducible. Explain that it contains three sets of squares with the side lengths respectively: $\frac{1}{2}$ unit, $\frac{1}{3}$ unit, and $\frac{1}{4}$ unit. (Note that the units are improvised units.) Students are to cut out the squares on the reproducible and use them to tile rectangles to show that the area found by tiling is the same as the area found by multiplying length times width.

4. Write the dimensions of the following three rectangles on the board:

   - Rectangle 1: 4 units long and $\frac{1}{2}$ unit wide. Students will use the $\frac{1}{2}$-unit squares to tile this rectangle.

   - Rectangle 2: 3 units long and $\frac{1}{3}$ unit wide. Students will use the $\frac{1}{3}$-unit squares.

   - Rectangle 3: 2 units long and $\frac{1}{4}$ unit wide. Students will use the $\frac{1}{4}$-unit squares.

5. Instruct your students to arrange the unit squares on their construction paper to create each rectangle. They should pay close attention to the dimensions. For example, for Rectangle 1, the length of 4 units is equal to eight $\frac{1}{2}$ units. Note that students will not need to use all of the squares in each set to tile each rectangle.

6. Explain that once they are sure the dimensions of the rectangle are correct, they should glue the squares on the paper to form a rectangle. They should then find the area of the rectangle by multiplying the number of tiles times the area of one tile, and confirm their answer by multiplying the length of the rectangle by its width.

CLOSURE

Discuss students' answers. Ask your students to explain the strategies they used to complete this activity. Will tiling a rectangle to find its area always equal the area found by multiplying its length times its width?

ANSWERS

The number of squares required to form each rectangle is listed, followed by the area of the rectangle. **(1)** Eight $\frac{1}{2}$-unit squares; $8 \times \frac{1}{4} = 2$ square units **(2)** Nine $\frac{1}{3}$-unit squares; $9 \times \frac{1}{9} = 1$ square unit **(3)** Eight $\frac{1}{4}$-unit squares; $8 \times \frac{1}{16} = \frac{1}{2}$ square unit.

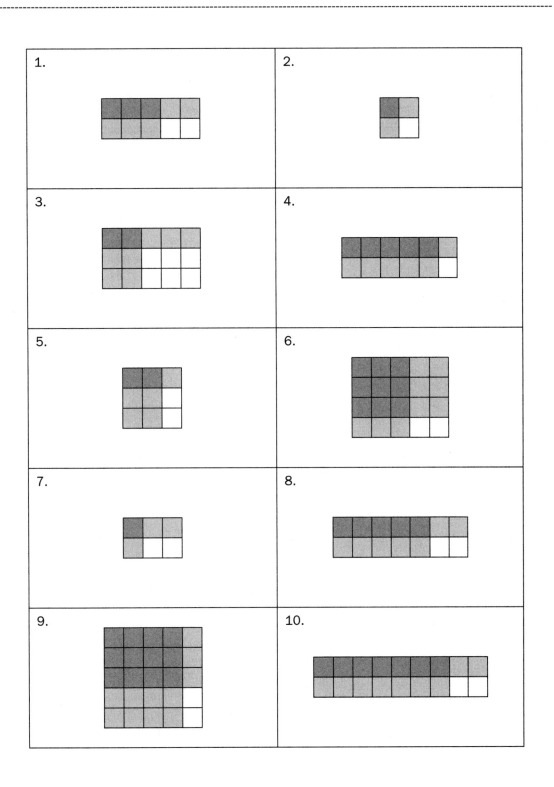

UNIT SQUARES FOR CONSTRUCTING RECTANGLES

$\frac{1}{2}$-unit squares

$\frac{1}{3}$-unit squares

$\frac{1}{4}$-unit squares

Number and Operations—Fractions: 5.NF.5

"Apply and extend previous understandings of multiplication and division to multiply and divide fractions."

5. "Interpret multiplication as scaling (resizing) by:

a. "Comparing the size of a product to the size of one factor on the basis of the size of the other factor, without performing the indicated multiplication.

b. "Explaining why multiplying a given number by a fraction greater than 1 results in a product greater than the given number (recognizing multiplication by whole numbers greater than 1 as a familiar case); explaining why multiplying a given number by a fraction less than 1 results in a product smaller than the given number; and relating the principle of fraction equivalence $\frac{a}{b} = \frac{(n \times a)}{(n \times b)}$ to the effect of multiplying $\frac{a}{b}$ by 1."

BACKGROUND

Multiplication is often thought of as a process of repeated addition of the same number that results in a number greater than the numbers multiplied. While this interpretation of multiplication works well for the counting numbers, it does not work for all numbers, particularly when multiplying a given number by a fraction less than 1. In this case, the product will be less than the given number.

Here is an example. If we multiply 3×4, we can easily see that this is the same as adding $4 + 4 + 4 = 12$. But when multiplying $4 \times \frac{1}{2}$, the product is 2, which is obviously less than 4.

Scaling, which can be thought of as resizing, addresses this problem. A number line can be used for illustrating this. Using the example of 3×4, think of 4 units that are stretched (resized) to be 3 times their original size. On the number line, the original 4 units will have the length of 12 units because they are scaled by a factor of 3.

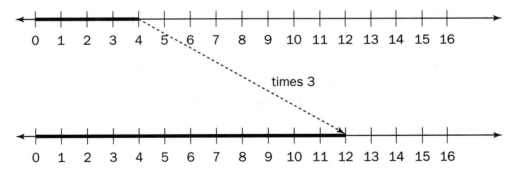

This method also works when multiplying a number by a fraction. Using the example of $4 \times \frac{1}{2}$, scaling $\frac{1}{2}$ by a factor of 4 results in 2.

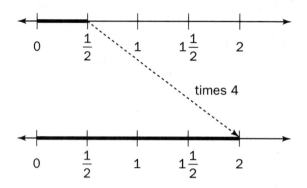

👥 ACTIVITY: SCALING NUMBERS FOR MULTIPLICATION

Working in groups, students will use a line segment to show an interpretation of scaling for multiplication.

MATERIALS

Rulers; crayons; colored pencils; unlined paper for each group.

PROCEDURE

1. Explain that although multiplication is often thought of as a process of repeated addition of the same number, a better way to think of multiplication is as a process of scaling, or resizing.

2. Explain the example and illustration of multiplying the whole numbers provided in the Background. Emphasize that multiplication in this case can be thought of as stretching a length of 4 units 3 times. This "stretching" is in fact resizing the original number. Once the 4-unit length is stretched 3 times, its length is 12 units. Note that the product is larger than the original number.

3. Now explain the example and illustration of multiplying the whole number and the fraction. Emphasize that when multiplying a number by a fraction less than 1, the product is less than the original number. Multiplying $4 \times \frac{1}{2}$ results in a product of 2.

4. Explain to your students that they are now to interpret multiplication as scaling. Present these two problems:

   - $6 \times \frac{2}{3}$
   - $2 \times 1\frac{1}{2}$

5. Suggest that students draw number lines divided into the number of equal units represented by the denominators of the fractions. They should use the number lines to interpret scaling of multiplication in a fashion similar to the examples you provided. They might prefer to use colors to highlight the resizing of numbers.

6. After completing their number lines and scaling, students should solve the problems by standard multiplication and compare their answers to the answers they found on their number lines.

CLOSURE

Instruct groups to write an exit ticket explaining why multiplying a given number by a fraction greater than 1 results in a product greater than the given number; and why multiplying a given number by a fraction less than 1 results in a product less than the given number.

ANSWERS

Number lines may vary but should be similar to the following:

(1)

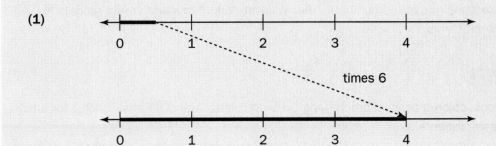

(2)

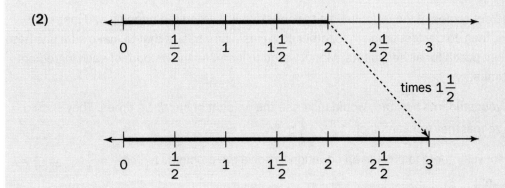

Number and Operations—Fractions: 5.NF.6

"Apply and extend previous understandings of multiplication and division to multiply and divide fractions."

6. "Solve real-world problems involving multiplication of fractions and mixed numbers, e.g., by using visual fraction models or equations to represent the problem."

BACKGROUND

Equations and models can help students understand and visualize mathematical processes. This is particularly true for multiplying fractions and mixed numbers.

 ACTIVITY: EXPANDING A RECIPE

Working in pairs or groups of three, students will solve problems involving a recipe by multiplying fractions and mixed numbers. They will write equations and create models to represent the problems.

MATERIALS

Rulers; crayons; colored pencils; graph paper; reproducible, "Mandi's Party Punch," for each pair or group of students.

PROCEDURE

1. Hand out copies of the reproducible to your students. Read the opening and instructions, then do the first problem together as a class. Emphasize that to make sure she has enough punch for all her guests, Mandi wants to increase the amount of each ingredient $1\frac{1}{2}$ times.

2. Ask your students how they would increase the amount of sugar $1\frac{1}{2}$ times. They should realize that they would multiply $1\frac{1}{4} \times 1\frac{1}{2}$ to find $1\frac{7}{8}$ cups.

3. Ask for volunteers to provide an equation to solve the problem. $1\frac{1}{4} \times 1\frac{1}{2} = \frac{5}{4} \times \frac{3}{2} = \frac{15}{8} = 1\frac{7}{8}$ cups.

4. Now ask your students to model this problem. Create the model as a class, using the images on the next page to draw the model on the board.

- Explain that $1\frac{1}{4}$ or $\frac{5}{4}$ is modeled below, showing 1 whole square and a quarter of another square. This represents the original amount of sugar.

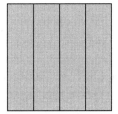 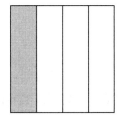

- To model $1\frac{1}{2}$ or $\frac{3}{2}$ (the expansion of the recipe), draw the previous model again, right below the original. This will result in 4 squares. Divide each square into 2 rows (which divides each square into 8 equal parts) and shade 3 of the rows. The 15 parts that are darkly shaded represent the product of $1\frac{1}{4}$ and $1\frac{1}{2}$, which is $\frac{15}{8}$ or $1\frac{7}{8}$.Remind your students that they are multiplying $\frac{5}{4}$ by $\frac{3}{2}$. Multiplying the denominators produces eighths.

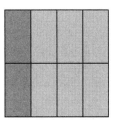 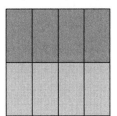

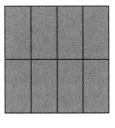 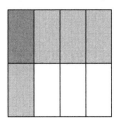

5. Explain that Mandi's punch recipe contains three more ingredients in addition to the sugar.

6. Explain that students are to increase the amount of each of the other three ingredients by $1\frac{1}{2}$. They are to write an equation and draw a model that represents the problem, and then solve the problem. They should show their work on the reproducible and draw their model on graph paper.

MANDI'S PARTY PUNCH

Mandi has invited her family for a party. She has a great recipe for party punch. To make sure she has enough punch, she wants to make more of the punch than the recipe calls for.

Directions: Write and solve an equation to find the amount of the ingredients Mandi must use if each ingredient is increased $1\frac{1}{2}$ times. Create a model that represents your multiplication.

1. $1\frac{1}{4}$ cups of sugar

2. $\frac{3}{4}$ cup of ginger ale

3. 3 pints of orange juice

4. $1\frac{3}{4}$ cups of water

Number and Operations—Fractions: 5.NF.7

"Apply and extend previous understandings of multiplication and division to multiply and divide fractions."

7. "Apply and extend previous understandings of division to divide unit fractions by whole numbers and whole numbers by unit fractions.

a. "Interpret division of a unit fraction by a non-zero whole number, and compute such quotients.

b. "Interpret division of a whole number by a unit fraction, and compute such quotients.

c. "Solve real-world problems involving division of unit fractions by non-zero whole numbers and division of whole numbers by unit fractions, e.g., by using visual fraction models and equations to represent the problem."

BACKGROUND

The process for dividing fractions includes the steps for multiplying fractions; however, the reciprocal of the divisor must be used to write the multiplication problem. Following are two examples:

- $\frac{1}{4} \div 2$: Rewrite 2 as an improper fraction, $\frac{2}{1}$, find its reciprocal, $\frac{1}{2}$, change the division sign to multiplication and multiply. $\frac{1}{4} \div 2 = \frac{1}{4} \div \frac{2}{1} = \frac{1}{4} \times \frac{1}{2} = \frac{1}{8}$

- $2 \div \frac{1}{3}$: Rewrite 2 as an improper fraction, $\frac{2}{1}$, find the reciprocal of $\frac{1}{3}$, which is $\frac{3}{1}$, change the division sign to multiplication and multiply. $2 \div \frac{1}{3} = \frac{2}{1} \div \frac{1}{3} = \frac{2}{1} \times \frac{3}{1} = \frac{6}{1} = 6$

 ACTIVITY: DIVIDING UNIT FRACTIONS

Working in pairs or groups of three, students will match word problem cards with cards containing the correct equation and solve each problem by modeling division.

MATERIALS

1 set of Cuisenaire rods; rulers; scissors; glue sticks; crayons; colored pencils; 9-inch-by-12-inch unlined paper; graph paper; reproducibles, "Division—Unit Fraction Cards, I" and "Division—Unit Fraction Cards, II," for each pair or group of students.

1. Work as a class and show your students how to model the examples in the Background using the Cuisenaire rods.

   - In the first problem, $\frac{1}{4} \div 2$, let the brown rod equal 1 whole, the purple rod equal $\frac{1}{2}$, and the red rod equal $\frac{1}{4}$. Tell your students to find two rods of the same color that, when put end to end, will equal the length of the red rod. They should find that two white rods equal the length of the red rod and this models $\frac{1}{4} \div 2$. To find the quotient, determine what the white rod represents compared to 1 whole. The white rod is $\frac{1}{8}$ of the whole or, in this case, the brown rod. $\frac{1}{8}$ is the quotient.

   - Explain that in the second problem, $2 \div \frac{1}{3}$, students must find a rod that can be divided into thirds. This time let the dark green rod equal 1 whole. To model this problem, students need 2 dark green rods because they are dividing 2 wholes. Ask students to find the rod that represents $\frac{1}{3}$ of the dark green rod. It is the red rod. You may want to remind students that in the last problem the red rod was equal to $\frac{1}{4}$. The red rod now represents a different fraction because a different color rod represents 1 whole. Instruct your students to find the number of red rods that when placed end to end will have the same length as the 2 dark green rods. Because 6 red rods equal the length of the 2 dark green rods, 6 is the quotient.

2. Remind your students that they are not limited to only using single rods to equal 1 whole. They can create a "train" of rods, for example 1 orange and 1 dark green together may equal 1 whole.

3. Hand out copies of the reproducibles. Explain that they contain 8 word problem cards and 8 equation cards, each of which represents one of the problems.

4. Explain that students are to cut out the problem cards and the equation cards, and match each word problem with its correct equation. Once they have matched a word problem with its equation, they are to glue the problem card and equation card on their unlined paper. They must then create a model of the problem on graph paper, cut their model out, and glue it beneath the problem on the unlined paper. Note that they may use Cuisenaire rods to help them create their models. Finally, they are to solve the equations.

CLOSURE

Check students' matched problems, equations, and models. Have students share their work and solutions with another pair or group. Discuss how models may vary and different models may represent the same problem.

ANSWERS

Models will vary but should represent the following answers. **(1)** $\frac{1}{2} \div 3 = n$; $n = \frac{1}{6}$
(2) $3 \div \frac{1}{2} = n$; $n = 6$ **(3)** $\frac{1}{5} \div 4 = n$; $n = \frac{1}{20}$ **(4)** $10 \div \frac{1}{2} = n$; $n = 20$ **(5)** $\frac{1}{8} \div 2 = n$; $n = \frac{1}{16}$
(6) $\frac{1}{4} \div 5 = n$; $n = \frac{1}{20}$ **(7)** $\frac{1}{2} \div 10 = n$; $n = \frac{1}{20}$ **(8)** $\frac{1}{3} \div 6 = n$; $n = \frac{1}{18}$

Problem Cards	Equation Cards
1. $\frac{1}{2}$ of a pizza pie is left. If 3 children want to share it equally, how much pizza will they each receive?	$\frac{1}{3} \div 6 = n$
2. Jillian has 3 yards of fabric that she will use to make bows for the school play. Each bow requires $\frac{1}{2}$ yard of fabric. How many bows can she make?	$\frac{1}{5} \div 4 = n$
3. A gallon container of apple juice is $\frac{1}{5}$ full. Four students will share equal amounts of the juice for snack time. What fraction of the gallon will each receive?	$\frac{1}{8} \div 2 = n$
4. Sam needs 10 feet of plastic border to place along a flower bed. The border comes in pieces that are $\frac{1}{2}$ foot long. How many pieces of border will he need?	$\frac{1}{2} \div 3 = n$

Problem Cards	Equation Cards
5. Dominic has a piece of string that is $\frac{1}{8}$ foot long. He is cutting it into 2 equal sections. How long will each piece be?	$10 \div \frac{1}{2} = n$
6. Joe wants to run a $\frac{1}{4}$-mile relay with 4 other students. How far will each student run during this race?	$\frac{1}{2} \div 10 = n$
7. $\frac{1}{2}$ of a large bag of candy will be shared equally among 10 students. How much will each student receive?	$3 \div \frac{1}{2} = n$
8. $\frac{1}{3}$ of a chocolate cake was left over. Joanna wanted to share it equally between her and 5 friends. What fraction of the cake will each person receive?	$\frac{1}{4} \div 5 = n$

Measurement and Data: 5.MD.1

"Convert like measurement units within a given measurement system."

> 1. "Convert among different-sized standard measurement units within a given measurement system (e.g., convert 5 cm to 0.05 m), and use these conversions in solving multi-step, real-world problems."

BACKGROUND

To convert from one unit of measurement to another within systems of measurement, students must be familiar with equivalent measures. Common measures are provided in the reproducible, "Measures," which you may distribute to your students if you feel it is necessary.

To convert from a larger unit to a smaller unit, students should multiply. For example, to change 300 minutes to seconds, multiply 300 by 60 because 1 minute equals 60 seconds. Therefore, 300 minutes = 18,000 seconds.

To convert from a smaller unit to a larger unit, students should divide. For example, to change 300 minutes to hours, divide 300 by 60 because 1 hour equals 60 minutes. Therefore, 300 minutes = 5 hours.

ACTIVITY 1: MEASUREMENT BINGO

Students will create a measurement bingo board by placing numbers from a Number Bank in each square on the board. The teacher will present a problem, requiring students to convert from one unit of measurement to another. If the answer is on the student's board, the student will cover the square that contains the answer with a counter. The first student to cover five squares in a row, column, or diagonal is the winner.

MATERIALS

24 1-inch diameter (or smaller) counters, reproducibles, "Measurement Bingo" and "Measures," for each student. Optional: One copy of reproducible, "Conversion Bank," for the teacher.

PROCEDURE

1. Distribute copies of the reproducibles. Explain that "Measurement Bingo" contains a bingo board and a Number Bank. "Measures" contains various measurements that students will find helpful when converting units of measurement for bingo.

2. Explain that students are to randomly fill in each square on their board with a number from the Number Bank. As they fill in a number, suggest that they cross out the number in the Number Bank so that they will not use the same number twice. Note that all numbers will be used to fill the board. They should not place a number in the free space.

3. Explain the rules of the game. You will present measurements that students must convert. The problems are contained on the reproducible, "Conversion Bank." (You may make a copy of this reproducible for yourself, or you may simply read the problems from that page in the book.) State the problems in order, starting with the first problem, and give students a few moments to convert the number to the specified unit. If they are correct, the answer will be on their board. Students who find the answer to the problem on their board should cover the square with a counter. Continue presenting problems until a student gets bingo by covering five squares in a row, column, or diagonal.

4. After a student announces she has bingo, check her answers to make sure that she is correct.

CLOSURE

Announce the correct answers and allow other students to make certain that their answers are correct, even though they may not have gotten bingo. Review any problems that students found confusing.

ANSWERS

(1) 7 (2) 5 (3) 400 (4) 12 (5) 21 (6) 9 (7) 64 (8) 730 (9) 3 (10) 48 (11) 24 (12) 4,000 (13) 8 (14) 120 (15) 1 (16) 10 (17) 300 (18) 6,000 (19) 6 (20) 4 (21) 108 (22) 500 (23) 2,000 (24) 2

 ## ACTIVITY 2: MEASUREMENT, CONVERSIONS, AND WORD PROBLEMS

Students will solve word problems that require them to convert units of measurement.

MATERIALS

Reproducibles, "Measures," and "Measurement Word Problems," for students.

PROCEDURE

1. Distribute copies of the reproducibles. Explain that "Measures" contains various measurements and conversions. If necessary, students should refer to this sheet to help them solve the five problems contained on "Measurement Word Problems."

2. Explain that whenever students solve word problems involving measurement, they should make sure that all units are the same.

3. Explain that when they convert from a larger unit to a smaller unit, they should multiply; when they convert from a smaller unit to a larger unit, they should divide.

4. Suggest that students write an equation to help them solve the problems. Note that some problems have more than one question.

5. Tell students that they should label their answers with the appropriate units.

CLOSURE

Discuss the answers as a class. Ask volunteers to explain any equations and strategies they used to solve the problems. Review any problems that students found difficult.

ANSWERS

(1) The height of 6 layers of cinder block is 48 inches, which equals 4 feet. (2) Danielle worked on her homework for 80 minutes. She was 10 minutes short of what she told her brother. (3) Lila had enough ribbon. She needed 150 centimeters and had 30 centimeters left over. (4) Mrs. Harper purchased enough juice. She had 4 cups left over. (5) Jacob should pack 4 liters of water, which is equivalent to 4,000 milliliters. Since each bottle contains 500 milliliters, he should pack 8 bottles.

MEASUREMENT BINGO

		Free Space		

Number Bank

1	2	3	4	5	6
7	8	9	10	12	21
24	48	64	108	120	300
400	500	730	2,000	4,000	6,000

1. 14,000 lb = ___ T	2. 5,000 m = ___ km	3. 4 m = ___ cm
4. 48 c = ___ qt	5. 3 wk = ___ days	6. 9,000 L = ___ kL
7. 4 lb = ___ oz	8. 2 yr = ___ days	9. 48 oz = ___ lb
10. 3 gal = ___ c	11. 2 ft = ___ in	12. 4 km = ___ m
13. 2 gal = ___ qt	14. 2 hr = ___ min	15. 1,000 mg = ___ g
16. 5 pt = ___ c	17. 5 min = ___ sec	18. 3 T – ___ lb
19. 2 yd = ___ ft	20. 48 in = ___ ft	21. 36 yd = ___ ft
22. 2 metric cups = ___ mL	23. 2 kg = ___ g	24. 20 mm = ___ cm

Length	
Customary Units	**Metric Units**
12 inches (in) = 1 foot (ft)	10 millimeters (mm) = 1 centimeter (cm)
3 ft = 1 yard (yd)	100 cm = 1 meter (m)
5,280 ft = 1 mile (mi)	1,000 mm = 1 m
1,760 yd = 1 mi	1,000 m = 1 kilometer (km)

Capacity	
Customary Units	**Metric Units**
8 fluid ounces (fl oz) = 1 cup (c)	1,000 milliliters (mL) = 1 liter (L)
2 c = 1 pint (pt)	250 mL = 1 metric cup
2 pt = 1 quart (qt)	4 metric cups = 1 L
4 c = 1 qt	1,000 L = 1 kiloliter (kL)
4 qt = 1 gallon (gal)	

Weight and Mass	
Customary Units (Weight)	**Metric Units (Mass)**
16 ounces (oz) = 1 pound (lb)	1,000 milligrams (mg) = 1 gram (g)
2,000 lb = 1 ton (T)	1,000 g = 1 kilogram (kg)

Time	
60 seconds (sec) = 1 minute (min)	365 days = 1 year (yr)
60 min = 1 hour (hr)	366 days = 1 leap year
24 hr = 1 day	10 yr = 1 decade
7 days = 1 week (wk)	100 yr = 1 century
Approximately 52 wk = 1 year	1,000 yr = 1 millennium

Name _____ Date _____

MEASUREMENT WORD PROBLEMS

Directions: Solve each problem.

1. Jason watched his father build a foundation for a new house. Jason's father told him that the foundation would have 6 layers of cinder blocks. Each cinder block was 8 inches high. How many feet high would the foundation be?

2. Danielle had a lot of homework last night. She did 20 minutes of math, 10 minutes of spelling, 25 minutes of science, and 25 minutes of social studies. She told her brother that she worked on her homework for $1\frac{1}{2}$ hours. Was she correct? If not, what was the difference in minutes of how long she really worked compared to what she told her brother?

3. Lila was wrapping two birthday presents for her brother. She estimated that she would need 70 centimeters of ribbon for one package and 80 centimeters of ribbon for the other package. She had 1.8 meters of ribbon. Did she have enough ribbon to wrap the package? If not, how much ribbon did she still need?

4. Mrs. Harper volunteered to bring juice for her daughter's class for the fifth grade picnic. She needed enough juice for 60 eight-ounce cups. She bought 4 gallons of juice. Would this be enough juice? If not, how much more juice did she need to buy?

5. Jacob and his father enjoy hiking. To prepare for their next hike, Jacob's father asked him to pack water. Jacob was to pack 2 liters of water for himself and 2 liters for his father. But when Jacob started to pack water bottles, he saw that each bottle contained 500 milliliters. How many bottles should Jacob pack in all for his father and himself?

Measurement and Data: 5.MD.2

"Represent and interpret data."

2. "Make a line plot to display a data set of measurements in fractions of a unit $\left(\frac{1}{2}, \frac{1}{4}, \frac{1}{8}\right)$. Use operations on fractions for this grade to solve problems involving information presented in line plots."

BACKGROUND

A line plot, also known as a dot plot, displays data along a number line. Each value of the data is marked with a symbol noting the frequency.

For example, a line plot displaying the lengths $3\frac{3}{8}, 4\frac{5}{8}, 5\frac{1}{4}, 5\frac{1}{2},$ and $5\frac{1}{2}$ is shown below.

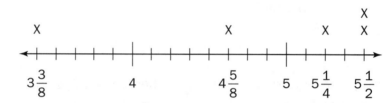

Note that an X is placed above the value each time the value appears.

ACTIVITY: LINE PLOTS AND PLANT HEIGHT

Students will create line plots that show the heights of bean plants. They will then answer questions based on their line plots. (*Note:* Although the data for this activity is provided, you may prefer to actually have your students grow bean plants and measure their growth. Suggestions for growing the plants are provided at the end of the activity.)

MATERIALS (IF STUDENTS ARE USING PROVIDED DATA)

Ruler with a $\frac{1}{8}$-inch scale; reproducible, "Bean Plant Growth," for each student.

PROCEDURE

1. Explain to your students that a line plot is a graph that shows the frequency of data along a number line. It is also called a dot plot. Present the example of the line plot provided in the Background. Because the largest denominator of the data is 8, the intervals between whole numbers are divided into eighths. The number line does not start at 0, but at $3\frac{3}{8}$,

which is the smallest value in this set of data. It ends with $5\frac{1}{2}$, which is the largest value. The frequency of the data is marked by an X above each value.

2. Explain that students will be creating a line plot that shows the height of bean plants three weeks after they were planted. You might note that the same kind of plants may grow at different rates due to a variety of factors, such as the amount of sunlight, temperature, amount of water, and type of soil.

3. Distribute copies of the reproducible. Explain that it contains data that shows the height of 30 bean plants that were planted three weeks ago. (*Note:* The heights are given as whole numbers, in eighths, in fourths, or in halves.) In some cases, students will have to recognize equivalent fractions, for example, $5\frac{1}{2} = 5\frac{4}{8}$. Near the bottom of the sheet is a line students are to use to draw their line plot.

4. Offer suggestions to help your students construct their line plots.

   - Find the smallest and largest values of the data.

   - Make a small vertical line on the line at the bottom of the reproducible to represent the smallest value. Place this vertical line at the beginning or near the beginning of the line. Place an X above this value above the number line.

   - Using a ruler and starting with the smallest value, mark off units at $\frac{1}{8}$-inch intervals. Stop at the number that represents the largest value, or stop a little beyond this number. Place an X above this value above the number line.

   - Label points on the number line for reference. Place an X every time a value is recorded. For example, if a value appears twice, two X's are required.

5. After your students have completed their line plots, pose questions such as the following:

   - What is the height of the tallest plant? $\left(6\frac{1}{2}\text{ inches}\right)$ What is the height of the shortest plant? $\left(3\frac{1}{4}\text{ inches}\right)$

   - What is the difference between the tallest plant and the shortest plant? $\left(3\frac{1}{4}\text{ inches}\right)$

   - If the height of the tallest plant was divided by 2, how tall would the plant be? $\left(3\frac{1}{4}\text{ inches}\right)$

   - What height appears most in the line plot? $\left(5\frac{1}{4}\text{ inches}\right)$ If a plant of this height were to double in size, how tall would it be? $\left(10\frac{1}{2}\text{ inches}\right)$

   - Find the sum of the heights of the three shortest plants. $\left(11\frac{3}{4}\text{ inches}\right)$

CLOSURE

Discuss students' line plots. Ask: How does this line plot help you to understand the data?

Heights of Bean Plants

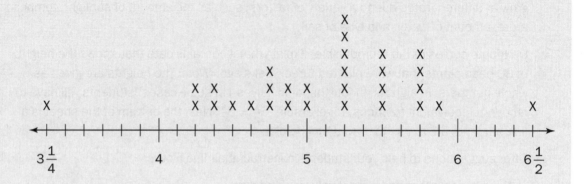

Note: Following are some suggestions should you decide to have students grow bean plants and measure their heights. **If you decide to do this, plant the seeds about three weeks before assigning the activity.** This will give them plenty of time to germinate and grow. Students may record the heights of the bean plants on reproducible, "Bean Plant Growth Class Data."

MATERIALS (FOR GROWING BEAN PLANTS)

Bean seeds; 14- to 16-ounce plastic cups (clear cups will allow students to see the root system of their plants); small plastic plates on which to place the cups; enough potting soil to fill each cup to about 1 inch from the top; water; an area where plants will receive sunlight; rulers with a $\frac{1}{8}$-inch scale; reproducible "Bean Plant Growth Class Data" for each student.

Some tips for growing the plants:

1. Poke a few holes in the bottom of each cup for drainage, then fill the cup with potting soil about 1 inch from the rim of the cup. Place the cup on the plastic plate and provide water until the soil is moist.

2. Place seeds in the cups, one seed per cup. The seeds should be planted about 1 to $1\frac{1}{2}$ inches deep in the soil. Cover the seeds with soil. Press the soil down firmly but gently.

3. Place cups along with their plates on a window sill (or other area) where they will receive ample sunlight.

4. Water the seeds regularly to make the soil moist, but not so much as to saturate the soil.

Plant	Height (in inches)	Plant	Height (in inches)	Plant	Height (in inches)
1	$5\frac{1}{2}$	11	$5\frac{1}{4}$	21	$4\frac{7}{8}$
2	$4\frac{3}{4}$	12	$5\frac{3}{4}$	22	$5\frac{1}{4}$
3	$4\frac{3}{8}$	13	5	23	$4\frac{1}{2}$
4	$5\frac{1}{2}$	14	$5\frac{1}{4}$	24	$3\frac{1}{4}$
5	$4\frac{7}{8}$	15	$5\frac{3}{4}$	25	$4\frac{3}{8}$
6	$5\frac{1}{4}$	16	$4\frac{1}{4}$	26	$5\frac{3}{4}$
7	$4\frac{1}{4}$	17	$5\frac{1}{2}$	27	$5\frac{3}{4}$
8	$4\frac{3}{4}$	18	$4\frac{5}{8}$	28	$5\frac{1}{4}$
9	$5\frac{7}{8}$	19	5	29	$5\frac{1}{2}$
10	$6\frac{1}{2}$	20	$4\frac{3}{4}$	30	$5\frac{1}{4}$

Heights of Bean Plants

Plant	Height (in inches)
1	
2	
3	
4	
5	
6	
7	
8	
9	
10	

Plant	Height (in inches)
11	
12	
13	
14	
15	
16	
17	
18	
19	
20	

Plant	Height (in inches)
21	
22	
23	
24	
25	
26	
27	
28	
29	
30	

Heights of Bean Plants

Measurement and Data: 5.MD.3

"Geometric measurement: understand concepts of volume and relate volume to multiplication and to addition."

3. "Recognize volume as an attribute of solid figures and understand concepts of volume measurement.

    a. "A cube with side length 1 unit, called a 'unit cube,' is said to have 'one cubic unit' of volume, and can be used to measure volume.

    b. "A solid figure which can be packed without gaps or overlaps using n unit cubes is said to have a volume of n cubic units."

BACKGROUND

Three-dimensional figures have length, width, and height. The volume, the amount of space inside the figure, is measured in cubic units.

    A rectangular prism has three pairs of congruent rectangular faces. The volume of a rectangular prism equals the number of cubes that are required to fill it, without any gaps between the cubes.

 ACTIVITY: BUILDING A RECTANGULAR PRISM

Working in pairs or groups of three, students will create a rectangular prism that has a volume of 16 cubic centimeters.

MATERIALS

16 1-centimeter cubes per pair or group of students.

PROCEDURE

1. Explain that the volume of a rectangular prism is the amount of space inside the prism. Note that a typical cardboard box is an example of a rectangular prism.

2. Explain that each 1-centimeter cube is 1 centimeter long, 1 centimeter wide, and 1 centimeter high. The volume of the cube is 1 cubic centimeter. Two cubes have a volume that equals 2 cubic centimeters, 3 cubes have a volume of 3 cubic centimeters, and so on.

3. Instruct your students to create rectangular prisms using all 16 of their centimeter cubes. They are to record the length, width, and height of each prism they create. Note that 16 centimeter cubes can be used to create 15 rectangular prisms, listed according to length, width, and height. Challenge your students to create all 15.

Discuss the dimensions of the prisms. Ask your students: How do you know that each prism has the same volume?

ANSWERS

The dimensions of the prisms are provided below.

Length	1	1	1	1	1	2	2	2	2	4	4	4	8	8	16
Width	1	16	8	2	4	1	8	2	4	1	4	2	2	1	1
Height	16	1	2	8	4	8	1	4	2	4	1	2	1	2	1

Measurement and Data: 5.MD.4

"Geometric measurement: understand concepts of volume and relate volume to multiplication and to addition."

> 4. "Measure volumes by counting unit cubes, using cubic cm, cubic in, cubic ft, and improvised units."

BACKGROUND

Volume, the amount of space in a container, can be found by counting the number of cubes that fill it. The product of the dimensions of the cube—length times width times height—times the number of cubes is equal to the volume of the container.

For example, if a container can be filled with 12 cubes, each having dimensions of 1 centimeter by 1 centimeter by 1 centimeter, the volume of the container is 12 cubic centimeters. If a container can be filled with 16 dice (an improvised unit), and each die has dimensions of $\frac{3}{4}$ inch by $\frac{3}{4}$ inch by $\frac{3}{4}$ inch, the volume of the container is $6\frac{3}{4}$ cubic inches. $16 \times \frac{3}{4} \times \frac{3}{4} \times \frac{3}{4} = 6\frac{3}{4}$

ACTIVITY: FINDING VOLUME

Working in pairs or groups of three, students will find the volume of rectangular prisms by counting the number of cubes that form them. They will then determine the actual volume by multiplying the number of cubes by the volume of each cube.

MATERIALS

100 1-centimeter cubes, 100 1-inch cubes, 100 $\frac{3}{4}$-inch dice (or $\frac{5}{8}$-inch dice or similar improvised unit) for a class of 30 students. (Smaller classes will require fewer cubes of each type.)

PREPARATION

Set up three work stations. Each station should have five desks. (You can use long tables instead of desks, but you should then divide each table into five sections.) Place 20 1-centimeter cubes on each of the five desks at one station. Place 20 1-inch cubes on each of the five desks at the second station. Place 20 $\frac{3}{4}$-inch dice on each of the five desks at the third station. This setup will easily accommodate a class of 30 students. (For smaller classes you may set up fewer work stations.) To make it easy for your students to find the proper station, label each station with a number and the type of cubes it contains, for example: "Station 1: 1-centimeter cubes."

1. Explain that volume refers to the space inside a container and that it is always measured in cubic units. For this activity, students will find the volume of rectangular prisms using three different-sized cubes.

2. Explain that three work stations are set up around the room. Each station has five desks. At one station, the desks contain centimeter cubes. At the second station, the desks contain inch cubes, and at the third station the desks contain dice, which are improvised units. The order of working at the stations does not matter, but students must work at all three stations. They will work at each station for about 10 minutes.

3. Explain that when they are at a station, they should work as pairs or in their groups and use the cubes to construct as many rectangular prisms as they can in the time allotted. Note that different pairs or groups of students may use different numbers of cubes to construct prisms with different dimensions. After students have completed a prism, they are to find the volume by multiplying the number of cubes by the volume of 1 cube. They are to record the dimensions and volume of each prism they construct.

4. After about 10 minutes, announce that students should move to a different station. They are to follow the same procedure with a different set of cubes. After another 10 minutes, students are to go on to the third station and follow the same procedure.

CLOSURE

Discuss students' results. Ask for volunteers to provide the dimensions, number of cubes, and volumes of some of the prisms they constructed. Instruct them to write an exit ticket explaining how the volume of a rectangular prism relates to the number of cubes and the dimensions of the cubes.

Measurement and Data: 5.MD.5

"Geometric measurement: understand concepts of volume and relate volume to multiplication and to addition."

5. "Relate volume to the operations of multiplication and addition and solve real-world and mathematical problems involving volume.

   a. "Find the volume of a right rectangular prism with whole-number side lengths by packing it with unit cubes, and show that the volume is the same as would be found by multiplying the edge lengths, equivalently by multiplying the height by the area of the base. Represent threefold whole-number products as volumes, e.g., to represent the associative property of multiplication.

   b. "Apply the formulas $V = l \times w \times h$ and $V = B \times h$ for rectangular prisms to find volumes of right rectangular prisms with whole-number edge lengths in the context of solving real-world and mathematical problems.

   c. "Recognize volume as additive. Find the volumes of solid figures composed of two non-overlapping right rectangular prisms by adding the volumes of the non-overlapping parts, applying this technique to solve real-world problems."

BACKGROUND

Although the volume of a rectangular prism can be found by counting the number of cubes that it contains, a far more practical way to find volume is to use one of the following formulas: $V = l \times w \times h$ where l stands for the length of the base, w stands for the width of the base, and h stands for the height of the prism; or $V = B \times h$, where B stands for the area of the base and h stands for the height. Because $l \times w$ is equal to the area of the base, the two volume formulas are equivalent. Regardless of the orientation of the prism, the volume is always the same.

 ## ACTIVITY 1: FINDING THE VOLUME OF A RECTANGULAR PRISM

Working in groups, students will fill a rectangular prism with centimeter cubes to find the volume. They will also find the volume of the rectangular prism by finding the product of the area of the base and the height.

MATERIALS

About 200 1-centimeter cubes; scissors; glue sticks; metric rulers; reproducible, "Rectangular Prism Net," for each group of students. (*Note:* The reproducible should be copied on card stock because it is sturdier than paper.) Optional: A cardboard box to show the dimensions of a rectangular prism.

PREPARATION

Make a copy of the net, contained on the reproducible, cut it out, and demonstrate the procedure for making the rectangular prism.

PREPARATION

1. Explain that the volume of a rectangular prism can be found by using formulas: $V = l \times w \times h$ or $V = B \times h$. Note what each variable represents. Also note that an example of a rectangular prism is a cardboard box. If you have a model of a rectangular prism, point out the dimensions to show what each variable represents.

2. Hand out copies of the reproducible. Explain that it contains a net, which is a figure that can be cut out and then folded to form a rectangular prism.

3. Instruct your students to cut out the net along the solid lines. Demonstrate how they should do this by working with your own figure. After cutting the net out, they should fold it along the dotted lines to form an "open" rectangular prism.

4. After students have formed the prism, they should glue its sides together where indicated on the tabs. Again, demonstrate this to students with your own prism.

5. Instruct your students to position their prisms so that the height is 4 centimeters. They are to then fill their prisms with centimeter cubes. Suggest that they place one layer of cubes at the bottom of their prism, and then count and record the number of cubes in that layer. They are to continue filling the prism by adding more layers. They should record the number of cubes in each layer.

6. After their prisms are filled, explain that students are to find the total number of cubes they used to fill the prism. Note that the number of cubes times the volume of each cube is equal to the volume of the prism.

7. Instruct your students to use metric rulers to measure the dimensions of the base of the prism and then find the area of the base by multiplying its length by its width. Next they should measure the height of their prism. Finally, they should use the formula, $V = B \times h$, to find the volume of the prism.

CLOSURE

Ask your students questions such as the following: How many 1-centimeter cubes did you need to fill your prism? (192) What is the volume of your prism? (192 cubic centimeters) What is the length of the base? (8 centimeters) What is the width of the base? (6 centimeters) What is the area of the base? (48 square centimeters) What is the height of the prism? (4 centimeters) How does the volume you found by packing cubes compare to the volume you found by multiplying the area of the prism's base by its height? (The volumes are the same.)

(*Note:* If you assign Activity 2 for this Standard, maintain the same groups and instruct students to keep their prisms.)

 ## ACTIVITY 2: USING FORMULAS TO FIND THE VOLUME OF RECTANGULAR PRISMS

Working in groups, students will use the rectangular prisms they constructed in Activity 1 to find the volume of a rectangular prism. (*Note:* If students did not complete Activity 1, they must construct the rectangular prism before starting this activity.)

MATERIALS

Rectangular prisms constructed previously; metric rulers for each group of students.

PROCEDURE

1. Explain that the volume of a rectangular prism can be found by multiplying the area of the base by the height. $V = B \times h$, where B stands for the area of the base and h stands for the height of the prism.

2. Remind students that the volume of the prisms they previously constructed was 192 cubic centimeters. The area of the base was 48 square centimeters (8 centimeters by 6 centimeters) and the height was 4 centimeters.

3. Instruct your students to position their prisms so that the base measures 6 centimeters by 4 centimeters. This will require them to turn their prisms and place them on their sides. Ask them to find the area of the base. (24 square centimeters) Ask them to find the height. (8 centimeters) Ask them to find the volume by multiplying the area of the base by the height of the prism. (192 cubic centimeters)

4. Now instruct your students to position their prisms so that the base measures 8 centimeters by 4 centimeters. Ask your students to find the area of the base. (32 square centimeters) Ask them to find the height of the prism. (6 centimeters) Ask them to find the volume by multiplying the area of the base by the height of the prism. (Volume = 192 cubic centimeters)

CLOSURE

Ask your students to write an explanation of how the formula $V = B \times h$ relates to the formula $V = l \times w \times h$. After they are done, ask volunteers to share their explanations. Students should realize that the formulas are equivalent because $l \times w$ equals the area of the base, which multiplied by the height equals the volume of the prism.

ACTIVITY 3: PACKING RECTANGULAR PRISMS

Working in groups, students will be given a cardboard box that they will fill with smaller boxes. They will find the total volume of the smaller boxes and the volume of the larger box. They will also find the volume of any unfilled space in the larger box.

MATERIALS

One cardboard box about 1 foot by 1 foot by 1 foot for each group; several small empty cardboard boxes; rulers; markers for each group.

PREPARATION

Obtain enough cardboard boxes measuring about 1 foot by 1 foot by 1 foot for each of your groups. Ask your students to bring in small, empty, clean cardboard boxes from home, for example cereal boxes, tissue boxes, tea bag boxes, pasta boxes, shoe boxes, and so on. Each group should have about 10 boxes of various sizes. To facilitate storage, store smaller boxes in larger ones. (*Note:* If groups have extra boxes, they may share them with other groups.)

PROCEDURE

1. Explain to your students that they are to fill the large cardboard box with smaller boxes, leaving the least amount of empty space.

2. Instruct your students to find the volume of their large box by measuring the dimensions of the box and then using either of these two formulas: $V = l \times w \times h$ or $V = B \times h$. After finding the volume of the large box, students should write the volume on the box.

3. Now instruct your students to find the volume of each smaller box, using the same procedure. They should write the volume on each box.

4. Explain that students are to fill the larger box with as many of the smaller boxes as possible without any boxes extending over the top of the large box. They should try to fill the large box so that no empty space (or as little space as possible) remains. If students are having trouble filling the large box, suggest that they find the sum of the volumes of various small boxes that might approximately equal the volume of the large box. This may help to reduce trial and error while filling the large box.

5. Tell your students that after they have found the sum of the volumes of the boxes that fit into the large box, they are to find the volume of any unfilled space.

6. If time permits, have students work with the boxes of another group and have the students compare their results.

CLOSURE

Discuss students' results. Ask questions such as the following: Did anyone have no unfilled space after packing the large box with the smaller boxes? If no group found this result, determine which group had the least amount of unfilled space. Did they try to rearrange the smaller boxes to reduce any unfilled space? Discuss why the sum of the volume of the smaller boxes might equal the volume of the large box but might not have fit inside the large box.

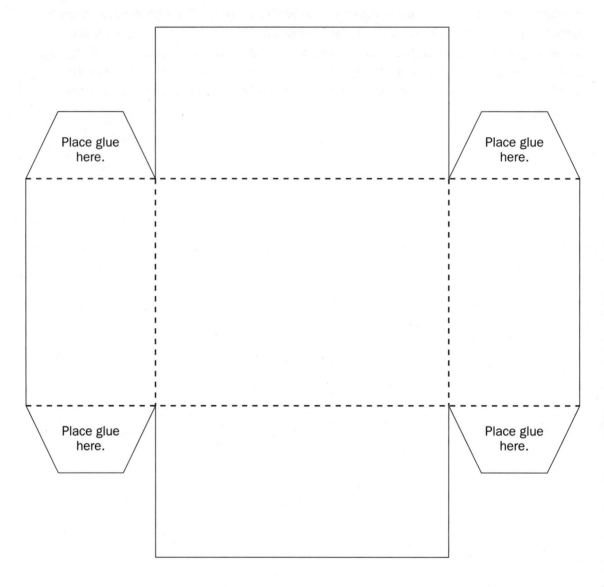

Place glue here.

Place glue here.

Place glue here.

Place glue here.

Geometry: 5.G.1

"Graph points on the coordinate plane to solve real-world and mathematical problems."

> 1. "Use a pair of perpendicular number lines, called axes, to define a coordinate system, with the intersection of the lines (the origin) arranged to coincide with the 0 on each line and a given point in the plane located by using an ordered pair of numbers, called its coordinates. Understand that the first number indicates how far to travel from the origin in the direction of one axis, and the second number indicates how far to travel in the direction of the second axis, with the convention that the names of the two axes and the coordinates correspond (e.g., x-axis and x-coordinate, y-axis and y-coordinate)."

BACKGROUND

The coordinate plane is created by the intersection of two perpendicular number lines. The horizontal line is called the x-axis, and the vertical line is called the y-axis. The point at which the lines intersect is called the origin, (0, 0). The axes divide the plane into four sections called quadrants. The quadrant in the upper right-hand section of the plane is Quadrant I. Moving in a counterclockwise direction, Quadrant II is the upper left-hand section of the plane, Quadrant III is the lower left-hand section, and Quadrant IV is the lower right-hand section.

Points can be plotted and located in the coordinate plane by using coordinates, or ordered pairs. An ordered pair is written in the form (x, y), where x is called the x-coordinate and y is called the y-coordinate. The x-coordinate tells how many spaces to move horizontally from the origin. The y-coordinate tells how many spaces to move vertically after moving horizontally.

ACTIVITY: CONSTRUCTING A COORDINATE PLANE

Students will construct a coordinate plane and locate specific points in it.

MATERIALS

Ruler; graph paper; reproducible, "Directions for Constructing a Coordinate Plane," for each student; overhead projector for the teacher.

PROCEDURE

1. Explain to your students that a coordinate plane is a flat surface formed by two perpendicular lines. The coordinate plane extends forever in all directions.

2. Hand out copies of the reproducible and explain that it contains directions for constructing a coordinate plane. Review the directions with your students to make certain that they understand the terms.

3. Instruct students to construct their coordinate planes. Caution them to follow directions precisely.

4. After your students have drawn their coordinate planes, identify the terms: horizontal line, vertical line, x-axis, y-axis, origin, and quadrants. Project a coordinate plane via an overhead projector to help your students follow your explanations.

5. Instruct your students how to plot points in the coordinate plane, for example, (5, 2). The first number represents the x-coordinate and the second number represents the y-coordinate. Explain that to plot points, students must begin at the origin.

They must move horizontally first, the number of places indicated by the x-coordinate.

- If the x-coordinate is positive (greater than 0), move to the right.
- If the x-coordinate is negative (less than 0), move to the left.
- If the x-coordinate is 0, stay at the origin.

Next they must move vertically from the x-coordinate, the number of places indicated by the y-coordinate.

- If the y-coordinate is positive, move up (from the point you stopped at on the x-axis). If the y-coordinate is negative, move down.
- If the y-coordinate is 0, stay there.

Mark the point and label the coordinates.

6. Instruct your students to plot the following points: (0, 2), (4, −1), (−2, 3) and (3, 5).

CLOSURE

Discuss the points students plotted. Ask for volunteers to use the overhead projector to find the points they plotted in the coordinate plane. Ask students to write the coordinates of four points of their own, then exchange their points for the points of a classmate. Students are to plot these points in their own coordinate planes, then check each other's work.

DIRECTIONS FOR CONSTRUCTING A COORDINATE PLANE

Follow these steps to construct a coordinate plane.

1. Find two perpendicular lines that intersect at or near the center of your graph paper. Using your ruler, draw two perpendicular lines on these lines. Put arrowheads at both ends of each line to show that the lines go on infinitely.

2. Mark the point at which the lines intersect with a dot. This point is called the origin. Label this point (0, 0).

3. Starting at the origin, move to the right. Number the first 10 vertical lines on your graph paper 1 through 10. Starting at the origin again, move to the left. Number the first 10 vertical lines on your graph paper −1 through −10. The horizontal line you moved along is called the x-axis.

4. Starting at the origin, move upward. Number the first 10 horizontal lines on your graph paper 1 through 10. Starting at the origin again, move downward. Number the first 10 horizontal lines on your graph paper −1 through −10. The vertical line you moved along is called the y-axis.

5. Points are always identified by two coordinates, for example, (3, 4). The first coordinate is the x-coordinate. It is plotted by moving along the x-axis. The second coordinate is the y-coordinate. It is plotted from the x-coordinate by moving along the y-axis or on a line parallel to the y-axis. Following are two examples:

   - To plot point (3, 4), start at the origin. Move 3 units to the right along the x-axis. Now move 4 units up, parallel to the y-axis. Mark this point and label it (3, 4).

   - To plot point (−1, −5), start at the origin. Move 1 unit to the left along the x-axis. Now move 5 units down, parallel to the y-axis. Mark this point and label it (−1, −5).

You have just plotted two points in the coordinate plane!

Geometry: 5.G.2

"Graph points on the coordinate plane to solve real-world and mathematical problems."

> 2. "Represent real-world and mathematical problems by graphing points in the first quadrant of the coordinate plane, and interpret coordinate values of points in the context of the situation."

BACKGROUND

The coordinate plane is formed by two perpendicular lines that divide the plane into four regions, called quadrants. In the first quadrant, the coordinates of the ordered pairs are positive numbers. The first quadrant of the coordinate plane serves as the basis for many graphs.

ACTIVITY: GRAPHING RELATIONSHIPS

Students will graph ordered pairs that show the relationship between the number of sides of two-dimensional figures and the number of their diagonals.

MATERIALS

Graph paper; reproducible, "Figures and Diagonals," for each student.

PROCEDURE

1. Review the coordinate plane with your students and focus their attention on the first quadrant. Note the *x*-axis, *y*-axis, and the origin. Also note that each point can be represented by an ordered pair, (*x*, *y*).

2. Explain that students are to graph the relationship between the number of sides of two-dimensional figures and the number of their diagonals. If necessary explain that a diagonal is a line segment drawn from one vertex to another non-adjacent vertex. Present the example of the rectangle below. It has four sides and two diagonals.

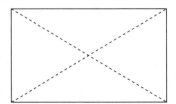

The number of sides can be represented by the *x*-coordinate, and the number of diagonals can be represented by the *y*-coordinate. The number of sides and diagonals for a rectangle can be represented as (4, 2).

3. Distribute copies of the reproducible. Explain that it contains five figures. Note that each has a different number of sides and a different number of diagonals. Students are to graph the relationship between the number of sides and the number of diagonals of each figure, representing the number of sides by the *x*-coordinate and the number of diagonals by the *y*-coordinate.

CLOSURE

Review students' graphs. Ask for volunteers to explain what each ordered pair represents. (The *x*-coordinate represents the number of sides of a figure; the *y*-coordinate represents the number of diagonals of a figure.)

ANSWERS

(**1**) triangle: 3 sides, 0 diagonals; (3, 0) (**2**) square: 4 sides, 2 diagonals; (4, 2) (**3**) pentagon: 5 sides, 5 diagonals; (5, 5) (**4**) hexagon: 6 sides, 9 diagonals; (6, 9) (**5**) heptagon: 7 sides, 14 diagonals; (7, 14)

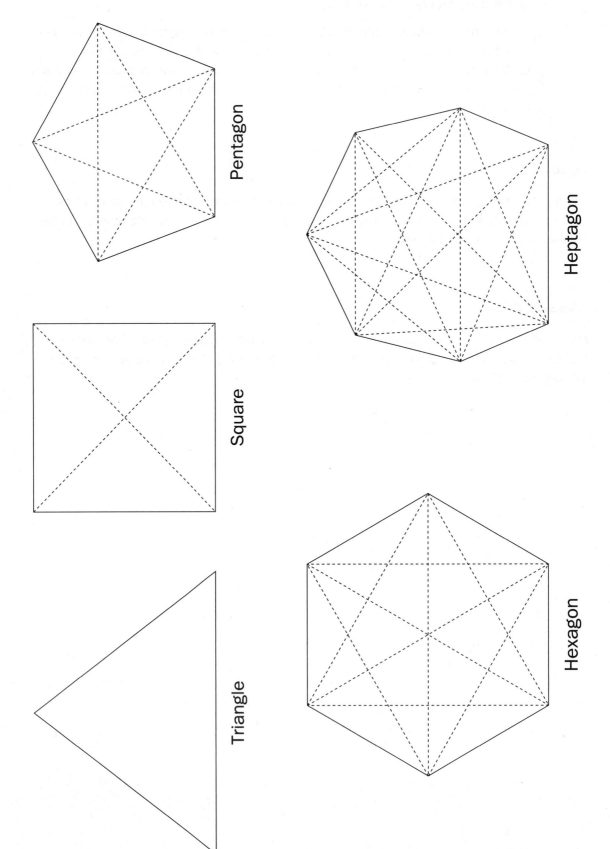

Pentagon

Heptagon

Square

Triangle

Hexagon

Geometry: 5.G.3

"Classify two-dimensional figures into categories based on their properties."

> 3. "Understand that attributes belonging to a category of two-dimensional figures also belong to all subcategories of that category."

BACKGROUND

Students sometimes think of two-dimensional figures as fitting into distinct categories. They fail to realize that some figures belong to subcategories.

Quadrilaterals are four-sided figures. If a quadrilateral has two pairs of parallel sides, it is a parallelogram. If a parallelogram has four congruent sides, it is a rhombus. If a parallelogram has four right angles, it is a rectangle. If a parallelogram has four congruent sides and four right angles, it is a square. Or, if a rectangle has four congruent sides, it is a square. If a rhombus has four right angles, it is a square. However, if a quadrilateral has exactly one pair of parallel sides, it is a trapezoid. It requires clear thinking and understanding on the part of students to classify two-dimensional figures into categories according to properties.

To help students understand the specific qualities of each type of quadrilateral, explain to them that *parallelogram* serves both as an umbrella term over an entire category (as just described) and as a specific example within that category, namely, a quadrilateral with two pairs of parallel and congruent sides but no right angles. Likewise *rhombus* can refer either to a category of parallelogram that has four congruent sides that might or might not have right angles, or to a specific type of parallelogram with four congruent sides but no right angles.

 ## ACTIVITY: NAMING QUADRILATERALS

Working in pairs or groups of three, students will categorize quadrilaterals so that all of the figures that have the same properties are placed together.

MATERIALS

Scissors; glue sticks; rulers; reproducibles, "Organizing Quadrilaterals" and "Quadrilaterals," for each pair or group of students.

PROCEDURE

1. Explain that quadrilaterals are two-dimensional figures that have four sides. The most common types of quadrilaterals are parallelograms, rectangles, rhombuses, squares, and trapezoids.

2. Hand out copies of the reproducibles. Explain that "Organizing Quadrilaterals" is divided into five sections: Parallelograms, Rectangles, Rhombuses, Squares, and Trapezoids. "Quadrilaterals" contains cards that show various quadrilaterals. Note that the cards are numbered from 1 to 10. Some cards, which will be used in more than one category, have the same number and figure.

3. Explain that students are to cut out the quadrilateral cards and glue them in their correct section on the organizer. Note that some sections will contain more cards than others.

4. Explain that because the figures on the cards are not named, students must pay close attention to their properties as shown on the card. Suggest that they use rulers to confirm congruent sides. Note that all right angles are shown with a box in the vertex.

CLOSURE

Check your students' results. Discuss how many figures are a subcategory of another figure and the properties that make them so.

ANSWERS

The card number is written after each figure. Parallelograms: 1, 2, 3, 5, 6, 7, 9, 10; Rectangles: 2, 3, 6, 7; Rhombuses: 3, 5, 6, 10; Squares: 3, 6; Trapezoids: 4, 8

Parallelograms

Rectangles

Rhombuses

Squares

Trapezoids

1.	2.	2.	3.
3.	3.	3.	4.
5.	5.	6.	6.
6.	6.	7.	7.
8.	9.	10.	10.

Geometry: 5.G.4

"Classify two-dimensional figures into categories based on their properties."

4. "Classify two-dimensional figures in a hierarchy based on properties."

BACKGROUND

Many two-dimensional figures may be arranged in a hierarchy based on their properties. In a hierarchy of two-dimensional figures, a figure below another is a special type of the figure above it. For example, every square is a special type of rectangle, but not every rectangle is a square.

ACTIVITY: A HIERARCHY OF TWO-DIMENSIONAL FIGURES

Working in small groups, students will create a poster showing a hierarchy of two-dimensional figures that includes quadrilaterals and triangles.

MATERIALS

Scissors; glue sticks; rulers; protractors; markers; crayons; colored pencils; construction paper; poster paper; reproducibles, "Polygon Hierarchy Pattern" and "Polygons: Definitions and Properties," for each group of students.

PROCEDURE

1. Explain that many two-dimensional figures share some properties. Offer the example of the square being a special type of rectangle, though not every rectangle is a square. A square has four right angles and four congruent sides; a rectangle has four right angles and two pairs of opposite, congruent sides. To help your students visualize these properties, show examples of squares and rectangles and discuss the properties of each.

2. Explain that students will create a poster that shows how various figures are related by sharing some properties. Students will create a hierarchy of polygons in which the figure below another is a special type of the figure above it.

3. Hand out copies of the reproducibles. Explain that "Polygon Hierarchy Pattern" contains a pattern that students can follow as a type of blueprint when making a hierarchy of polygons on their posters. Each balloon should be replaced with a figure that is included on "Polygons: Definitions and Properties." You might, however, suggest that students create their own patterns.

4. Explain that students are to draw the figures that they will use to complete a hierarchy of polygons on construction paper, cut them out, and then glue them in a hierarchical pattern on their poster paper. They should use rulers and protractors to ensure the accuracy of their figures. They are to label each figure on their poster and write each figure's properties below it.

5. Encourage your students to be creative with their hierarchical posters but also be mathematically accurate.

CLOSURE

Have students share their posters with other groups. Discuss the hierarchical pattern of polygons and why a figure below another figure is a special type of that figure. What are their common properties? Display the posters.

ANSWERS

Names instead of actual figures are provided.

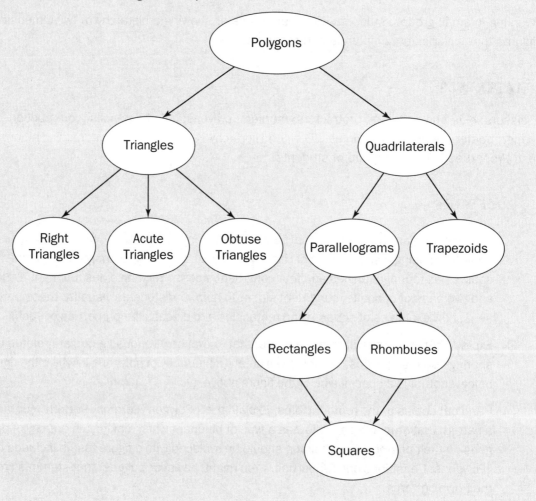

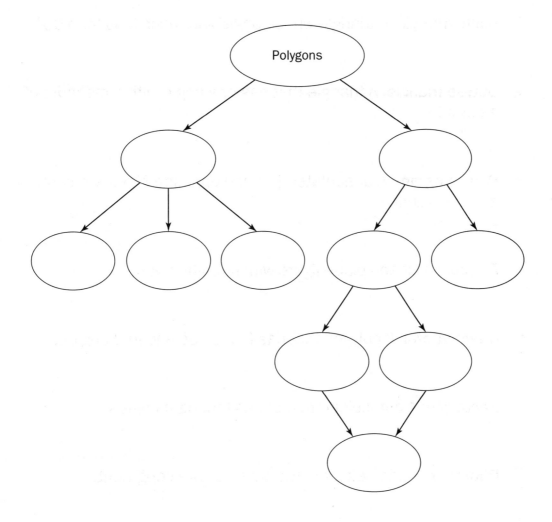

1. **Acute triangle:** A triangle whose angles are each less than 90°.

2. **Obtuse triangle:** A triangle that has one angle with a measure of greater than 90°.

3. **Parallelogram:** A quadrilateral whose opposite sides are parallel and congruent.

4. **Polygon:** A closed plane figure with straight sides.

5. **Quadrilateral:** A polygon that has four sides and four angles.

6. **Rectangle:** A parallelogram that has four right angles.

7. **Rhombus:** A parallelogram whose sides are congruent.

8. **Right triangle:** A triangle that has one angle of 90°.

9. **Square:** A rectangle that has four congruent sides.

10. **Trapezoid:** A quadrilateral that has exactly one pair of parallel sides.

11. **Triangle:** A polygon that has three sides and three angles.

INDEX

C

Charting Patterns in Powers of 10 activity (Grade 5), 188–189

Classifying Quadrilaterals activity (Grade 3), 72–74

Classroom Line Symmetry activity (Grade 4), 172

Color the Multiples activity (Grade 3), 24–26

Combining Groups activity (Grade 3), 2

Comparing Fractions activity (Grade 4), 115–117

Complete the Rows activity (Grade 4), 128–129

Completion Cards form (Grade 4), 129

Composite numbers: more than two factors of, 89; that are less than 100, 89

Constructing a Coordination Plane activity (Grade 5), 257–259

Conversion Bank form (Grade 5), 239

Coordination system: four quadrants of, 257; represent problems by graphing points in first quadrant of, 260–262; use perpendicular number lines (axes) to define, 257–259

Covering the Area activity (Grade 3), 57–58

Creating Numbers activity (Grade 5), 190–192

D

Data representation and interpretation: hand spans used for, 54–56; line plots used for (Grade 3), 54–56; line plots used for (Grade 4), 151–154; line plots used for (Grade 5), 242–246; picture graphs and bar graphs used for, 52–53

Decimal Battle activity (Grade 4), 140–141

Decimal Battle Cards form (Grade 4), 141

Decimals: compare two decimals to hundredths by reasoning about their size, 139–141; decimal notation for fractions with denominators 10 or 100, 134–138; modeling multiplication and division of, 205–206; place value, addition, and subtraction of, 204–205, 207–208; read, write, and compare decimals to thousandths using place value, 190–192; understood for fractions and comparing decimal fractions, 130–133

Decomposing a Fraction activity (Grade 4), 118–119

Decomposing Angles activity (Grade 4), 160–163

Decomposing Areas activity (Grade 3), 65–66

Decomposing Figures activity (Grade 3), 75–79

Demonstrating Division activity (Grade 4), 109–110

Designing a Vegetable Garden activity (Grade 3), 69–71

Directions for Constructing a Coordinate Plane form (Grade 5), 259

Dividends: definition of, 200; Demonstrating Division activity to find, 109–110; Dividends and Quotients form on, 112; Division Puzzles activity to find, 110–112; Finding Dividend, Divisors, and Quotients form, 203; Piecing Together Division activity on, 200–201, 203

Dividends and Quotients form (Grade 4), 112

Dividing Unit Fractions activity (Grade 5), 231–234

Division: apply properties of operations as strategies for, 10–12; combining whole number groups using, 2; determining the unknown whole number in equation, 8–9; finding whole-number quotients and remainders using, 109–112; fluently multiply and divide within 100, 17–20; matching word problems with equations, diagrams, and answers, 4–7; modeling multiplication and division of decimals, 205–206; relate area to operations of multiplication and, 63–66; representing and solving problems involving, 3; to solve word problems involving multiplicative comparison, 84–85; understood as an unknown-factor problem, 13–16

Division Puzzles activity (Grade 4), 110–112

Division–Unit Fraction Cards, I form (Grade 5), 233

Division–Unit Fraction Cards, II form (Grade 5), 234

Drawing Geometric Figures activity (Grade 4), 164–165, 167

Drawing Geometric Figures form (Grade 4), 167

Drawing Two-Dimensional Figures activity (Grade 4), 168–170

E

Equation Bank form (Grade 3), 9

Equation Tic-Tac-Toe activity (Grade 3), 8–9

Equations: determining the unknown whole number in, 8–9; finding whole-number quotients and remainders using, 109–112; interpreting multiplication equation as a comparison, 82–83; matching word problems with, 4–7; multiplication of fractions and mixed numbers using, 228–230; Problems, Models, and Equations activity (Grade 4), 120–126; solving word problem by using visual fraction models or, 217–218; Two-Step Equations, 23

Equations and Problems activity (Grade 4), 86–88

Estimating, Adding, and Subtracting Fractions form (Grade 5), 216

Modeling Multiplication activity (Grade 5), 196–197

Modeling Multiplication and Division of Decimals activity (Grade 5), 205–206

Modeling Multiplication of Fractions activity (Grade 5), 220, 223

Multi-digit arithmetic: find whole-numbers quotients and remainders to perform, 109–112; fluently add and subtract within 1,000, 30–33; multiply one-digit whole numbers by multiples of 10, 34–36; multiplying whole numbers using properties of operations and place value, 106–108; use place value understanding to perform, 106–108; use place value understanding to round whole numbers, 27–29

Multi-Digit Multiplication Quiz (Grade 5), 199

Multi-digit whole numbers: find whole-number quotients of, 200–203; fluently add and subtract using the standard algorithm, 103–105; fluently multiply using standard algorithm, 196–199; perform operations with decimals to hundredths and, 204–208; properties of operations and place value used for multiplying, 106–108; read, write, and compare multi-digit whole numbers, 97–99; recognizing different values in, 184–187; understanding place value for, 94–96; use place value understanding to perform, 106–108; use place value understanding to round, 100–102. *See also* Whole numbers

Multiplication: apply properties of operations as strategies for, 10–12; combining whole number groups using, 2; described as a comparison between the product and its factors, 82; determining the unknown whole number in equation, 8–9; finding whole-number quotients and remainders using, 109–112; fluently multiply and divide within 100, 17–20; fluently multiply multi-digit whole numbers using standard algorithm, 196–199; fraction equivalence used to solve work problems involving, 214–216; identifying patterns of, 24–26; interpreting a multiplication equation as a comparison, 82–83; matching word problems with equations, diagrams, and answers, 4–7; modeling multiplication and division of decimals, 205–206; of multi-digit whole numbers based on place value and properties of operations, 106–108; multiply a fraction by a whole number, 127–129; relate areas to the operations of division and, 63–66; representing and solve problems involving, 3;

scaling (resizing) for, 225–227; to solve word problems involving multiplicative comparison, 84–85; solving volume problems by relating volume to addition and, 251–256; thought of as process of repeated addition, 226; understand division as an unknown-factor problem and relationship to, 13–16; world problems involving time intervals in minutes, 45–46

Multiplication and Division Bingo activity (Grade 3), 17–20

Multiplication and Division Bingo form (Grade 3), 19

Multiplication of Fractions form (Grade 5), 223

Multiplication Table form (Grade 3), 26

Multiplication Tic-Tac-Toe activity (Grade 4), 82–83

N

Naming Quadrilaterals activity (Grade 5), 263–266

Number and operations–Fractions (Grade 3): explain equivalence of fractions in special cases and comparing fractions by size, 41–44; understanding fraction as number on the number line, 39–40; understanding how a fraction quantity is formed, 37–38

Number and operations–Fractions (Grade 4): compare two decimals to hundredths by reasoning about their size, 139–142; compare two fractions by creating common denominators or numerators, 115–117; express a fraction with denominator 10 as equivalent fraction with denominator 100, 130–133; multiply a fraction or whole number by a fraction, 127–129; understand a fraction as a sum of fractions, 118–126; use decimal notation for fractions with denominators 10 or 100, 134–138; use visual fraction models to explain equivalent fractions, 113–114

Number and operations–Fractions (Grade 5): add and subtract fractions with unlike denominators, 209–213; divide unit fractions by whole numbers and whole numbers by unit fractions, 231–234; interpret fraction as division of the numerator by the denominator, 217–218; interpret multiplication as scaling (resizing), 225–227; multiplication of fractions and mixed numbers, 228–230; multiply a fraction or whole number by a fraction, 219–224; solve word problems using equivalent fractions to add and subtract, 214–216

masses of objects, and intervals of time, 47–51; Measurement, Conversions, and Word Problems activity, 236–237, 240–241; multiply or divide problems involving multiplicative comparison, 84–85; solve equivalent fractions to add and subtract fractions, 214–216; solve multistep problems posed with whole numbers, 86–88; visual fraction models used to solve, 217–218

Word Problems with Measurement activity (Grade 4), 144–146

X

x-axis, 257–258

Y

y-axis, 257–258

Z

Zero: multi-digit arithmetic and understanding of, 30–33; *A Place for Zero: A Math Adventure* (LoPresti), 30